UNCOVERING THE INNER HERO

WAKE UP, OWN YOUR LIFE, AND MANIFEST YOUR ULTIMATE POTENTIAL

JONATHON CALHOUN DUGAN

Oxygen PUBLISHING AGENCY
AUTHORITY BY THE BOOK

Uncovering the Inner Hero

Jonathon Calhoun Dugan

1st Edition. 1st printing 2021

Cover Design & Interior Design: Steve Walters, Oxygen Publishing Inc.

Cover and Interior Illustrations by: Orfinart

Editor: Richard Tardif

Author Photo: Mackenna Dayton

Independently Published by
Oxygen Publishing Inc.
Montreal, QC, Canada
www.oxygenpublishing.com

ISBN: 978-1-990093-31-9

Imprint: Independently published

DEDICATION

To the ones who have yet to uncover their Inner Hero.

The time has come.

The world needs you.

TABLE OF CONTENTS

PREFACE

Are you living your best life? Take a breath. Soften your heart. Be honest. If today is your last day on earth, did you live the life you wanted? Did you take risks toward your dreams? Did you challenge yourself to be better in as many areas of life as you could? Have you traveled to the exotic places on your bucket list? Did you live a full life? Or did you play it "safe"? Would you die with unfulfilled desires and potential, dormant inside of you?

Are you living your life as the hero of your story or slowly dying? Is your body moving through the motions while your soul is sleeping? When you are honest with yourself, you may face some hard realities. Are you self-sabotaging, limiting, and not fully loving yourself in the ways you are capable of? There is still time to change, no matter where you are in life. It's not too late to wake up.

Socrates, over 2400 years ago (514a–520a) in his work *Republica,* wrote *Plato's Cave,* a story that is as fitting today as it was in his time. A group of people were born deep underground in a cave and chained so they could only look in one direction, forcing them to stare at a wall of rock their entire lives. There was no natural light, and it was damp and dark. They were born imprisoned without knowing it. There was a walkway behind them where people and animals would travel, and on the other side of the walkway was a fire. This fire cast shadows on the wall in front of the prisoners. They would name the images. They believed these shadows were reality. The better they got at recognizing and naming these shadows the more successful they were at life.

One day, one prisoner found himself outside of the cave, and free. The light from the sun was overwhelmingly bright. The man could not open his eyes, as you can imagine what happens to you after a friend swiftly flips the switch to turn on the lights after being in a dark room. At first, the light pained him. Slowly, he adjusted by first looking down at the ground. He could recognize some shadows from the trees and the animals. Soon, he realized the source of the shadowy objects. He saw the beauty of the trees, the exotic colors of the flowers, the majestic being of the horse, the vastness of the sky, and eventually grew conscious that the only reason he could see any of it was because of the ultimate source of light, the sun.

He reflected on his life in the cave and how he would perceive the shadows on the wall as reality, concluding that he was living within an illusion. His newfound awareness gave him the understanding that there were higher levels of existence. He wanted to help the other prisoners come to this expanded realization. To his surprise, when he returns, he goes into the cave to tell his fellow prisoners what he had experienced, and they each deny his truth. They became angry and aggressive toward him and didn't want to be convinced of this higher form of reality, because the cave is the only reality their mind has ever known. They were willing to fight for the beliefs and life passed down to them from previous generations, instead of adopting this new way of living.

There are countless ways of interpreting this story. I see the people in *Plato's Cave* split into the ones who wake up to consciousness and the ones who remain unconsciously asleep. Today, we compare *Plato's Cave* to the 1999 movie *The Matrix*. The prisoners in the cave have taken the blue pill, and the one who escaped took the red pill. When our prisoner left the cave, he was pulled out, or stepped out of the program. It took time to find his balance in this new reality of a higher existence. Eventually, he saw the truth. The light showed him this truth.

I was alone outside of the cave years ago, after a tragedy showed up in my life. I woke up, took ownership of my life, manifested the potential inside of me, and saw the light by uncovering the Inner Hero. I lost people along the way when I returned to my cave to explain my new awareness. They didn't have the ears to hear. These moments left me questioning myself, but the more I explored my inner world, the more I gained clarity.

I found that my previous reality was only the illusion of the shadows reflecting from my inner beliefs. I eventually found a tribe that had become conscious of their Inner Hero. After years of connecting with everyday heroes, sharing with them my intensive transformation to become the person who I am today, I left them in awe. They encouraged me to write my story to share with others who are waking up, who are becoming conscious, and who desire more out of life—the ones who need this story to move them forward to connecting deeper with their Inner Hero.

My story is messy, yet without the messiness, I wouldn't know the blissfulness of the moments when I am completely present and whole. It feels as if I have arrived.

But did I truly arrive, or did I just wake up in another cave? There are caves within caves within caves. Our work is to continue to wake up from the limits we place on ourselves. This is what it means to be an enlightened or conscious being. We are always arriving at the evolution of our journey. My story will help guide you to a space of continued arrival. This is just the beginning. Awareness is key.

Socrates also wrote, "The only true wisdom is knowing you know nothing."

I had to look at all of my insecurities, inadequacies, unworthiness, and my dark spaces to uncover the Inner Hero. I encourage you to do the same. You'll experience surprise at what wisdom awaits. You were created from greatness to be great. The time is now to receive what you have been searching for. Step into your greatness. If not now, then when?

INTRODUCTION

Y ou're here for a reason, where you're supposed to be. It's not an accident that you are reading this book. Are you ready to meet your hero? You don't know it yet, but that hero is you. You don't understand how to uncover the Inner Hero—not yet—but you will.

We have all hoped for a hero to save us from life's hardships. It's why we can't help gravitating toward superhero action films to root for the underdog, to lean in when a radioactive spider or a lightning strike in an instant transforms the underdog into a superhero, bursting with courage and shining light. We recognize this hero because he's walked through the depths of sorrow, darkness, loneliness, and broken-heartedness. Maybe you feel like the underdog, lost at sea amid violent storms, wandering through the wilderness without a map, feeling unwanted, unworthy, and uncertain? Then one day, you gaze into the mirror and realize the hero is you.

This book will help you uncover your Inner Hero.

Mahatma Gandhi said, "We must be the change that we wish to see in the world." That means we must do the work. By doing the work, we then understand the Inner Hero formula. We must first break out of being the victim of life. The more we tap into our Inner Hero, the closer we become to being the hero in the movie of our life.

But we don't need heroes saving the world. We need the bravery to carry out the most arduous work that we can do, to explore less the physical world but the world that exists between your ears and behind your eyes, the inner mind, the most potent and intricate reality in existence.

Here is where heroes exist.

We need to see through the illusions of our lived experiences, traumas, belief systems, and core programming.

Here is where heroes live.

We must learn, develop, and align with the all-loving, collective connectedness, the oneness of all things, the source of existence, our internal powers.

Here is where heroes thrive.

We integrate this energy within, and bind every cell and particle that exists in you and this universe. You can open up and connect with this energy. Star Wars calls this the Force, and some call it Prana, the Holy Spirit, God, Angels, Guides, Source Energy, the Universe, or the Great Spirit. This part of yourself is always with you.

What if I said you could open up to this part of yourself, and by doing so, you become more present, joyful, empowered, loving, and fulfilled in your life? Well, you can, and you will, if you follow the principles in this book. Develop the powers within, and let go of the judgments about what the outside world has trained you to believe about yourself and your potential. The more you develop and connect to your inner world, the more you make a difference in the external world. You might be a coach, maybe a healer, or a mother, a father, brother, a sister, a son, a daughter, a teacher, or a student? The title you place on yourself doesn't matter. You are someone who's here for a purpose.

To understand what it takes to save ourselves, love ourselves, forgive ourselves, honor ourselves, take responsibility for our life; we can change our inner world by owning our reality, becoming the hero in our life first. It's up to us to save ourselves. No more looking around for people, things, money, or anything external to fix your life. It's time for you to take the reins and be the driver of your reality. Everything you need is inside of you.

The greater part of yourself, the true nature of who you are, has called you to this moment to experience a powerful transformation. You are ready to own your reality and become the hero you have been looking for. This metamorphosis is that of the caterpillar transforming into the butterfly. You are a butterfly, not a caterpillar. You are ready for change. The world is ready.

•

I've been there.

I've walked through the deepest depths of sorrow, darkness, loneliness, and broken-heartedness. I was lost at sea amid those deadly storms, wandering through the wilderness without a map, feeling unwanted, unworthy, uncertain, and labelled as average.

To fit in, I played the game of life. I played team sports, winning State Championships, an introvert with extreme social anxiety winning a Gold Medal in the Junior Olympics. I was the insecure yet popular kid in school, even a Homecoming King. I got married at a young age, creating the all-American dream of a white picket fence lifestyle. I had a beautiful wife, a $100K a year job, traveled to 19 countries, and even had a perfectly behaved labradoodle. Yeah, life seemed great for this hero, right?

I considered myself hopelessly average. I was a boy afraid to be seen, to be heard, loved, and terrified of the thought of being rejected. I took every step with a smile, uncomfortable and afraid to show others any emotion. I did what I could to morph into the surrounding people, to feel even the slightest acceptance, and have them feel proud of me.

Then something happened.

I discovered that we only have this one life, this one-go-around, and it changed how I saw myself, the surrounding people, God, and my life's purpose. Change sounds amazing, but it's painful too. If you have ever watched the Matrix, you understand that Neo, the movie's main character, woke up to a world of chaos after swallowing the red pill. He had to unlearn his previous life's programming and then relearn who he was. It was a painful and challenging journey for him to become the One.

I woke up. That would be the best thing possible, right? But everything around me fell apart. I fell in and out of depression, consumed by unworthiness and never being enough. I lost loved ones. There were moments when I felt like I was living in prison, crushed by the weight of the darkness, lost, alone, uncertain, and afraid, again in the wilderness with no way out.

I realized I was not aligning with my Inner Hero. Through the growing pains that came with breaking out of my false identities, I eventually became the hero of my story. I credit faith, persistence, and grit. It was not from getting struck by lightning or getting bit by a radioactive spider.

My journey was a messy one in which I fell repeatedly, and through that, I built up resilience and strengthened my internal powers.

The hardships, trials and tribulations, lessons, successes, and Moments of AHA! changed my life. These are moments of awakening. How I showed up in the world became different from how I lived in the past, a split in time. I've had multiple life-altering experiences, and from those I know that I'm here not to save the world, but to save myself first.

•

My Inner Hero wrote this book so that you can meet your Inner Hero.

I promise that when you align with that greater part of yourself, your life will change. It might not be overnight, but with consistency, openness, surrender, discipline, and self-love; then you will transform into the hero in your life. You will feel joyful, empowered, and fully alive.

Uncovering the Inner Hero is a practical approach to self-exploration, self-discovery, self-love, and self-healing. By developing and uncovering this part inside yourself, you will attract more clients, more money, more happiness, more health, more love, more laughter, more connection to others, and more eagerness and excitement for life. You'll feel more empowered than you have ever felt before, and you will be a complete version of yourself.

This book gives you a Transformational AHA!, a profound mental, emotional, and transformational spiritual experience, which causes you to shift behaviors toward a positive and empowering direction. You can accomplish this by being open to thinking differently, letting go of the outdated beliefs that no longer serve you, stepping out of your comfort zone, upgrading your self-narrative, and doing the best you can by playing all out.

Apply the methods, do the exercises, and embody and integrate what you learn in this book through repetition. You will inevitably align with the version of yourself who is the hero in your life.

Together, we will change the world, but first we must start with the hero in the mirror. I believe in you. You are meant to be seen, to be heard, and to be loved. You are greatness. You are enough, and you can have, do and be whoever you desire.

It's time.

PART 1

DEATH IS JUST THE BEGINNING

CHAPTER 1
ISYMFS

"It's Still Your Mother Fucking Set!"
CT Fletcher

If you've never heard this phrase, stop reading.

I need you to look up, "It's Still Your Mother Fucking Set" (ISYMFS) by CT Fletcher on YouTube. It's a short video, but damn, it's powerful if you allow it to sink in and implement this mindset into your life during hard times.

I learned about ISYMFS during one of the most challenging times in my life, a period where I had died, not physically, but it certainly felt that way. I died mentally and emotionally, consumed by the heaviness of grief—the dark side of my transformation, a time that split and changed everything in my life.

This was the first time that I had ever questioned my existence. Why was I here? Why are we all here? There wasn't any reason I would or even should question life. I was a happy-go-lucky motherfucker with a smile plastered on my face 95% of the time, a mask I wore so people didn't have to worry about, "What's going on with Jonathon?" People don't have to worry about happy people, even if it's a lie.

I was always smiling because when I was young, I would squint my face when I was concentrating on something, which made everyone around me think I had this goofy smile. Kids would always ask, "Why are you always smiling?" I would repeatedly tell them, "I'm not smiling. That's just how I look." Some people have "Resting Bitch Face Syndrome" but I had "Resting Happy Face Syndrome."

Still, life was working out for me. I had no grounds for complaints. I was a good people pleaser, a superb athlete from the age of seven, chosen as captain on every team. I won a high school State Championship in football and volleyball, won a gold medal in volleyball at the Junior Olympics, and was honored with the MVP award.

I married at 22 to a beautiful and intelligent woman, attended church on Sundays, held a six-figure job, bought my first home at 23, and by 25 I had traveled to 19 countries. I had a loving and supportive family and amazing friends.

CHAPTER 2
THE PROGRAM

I had a life that anyone would die for. I felt blessed. What did I have to complain about? I had created the life of the white picket fence family. Wasn't that the goal? Wasn't that expected? Isn't this the program? When I say, "program," I'm referring to the construct of how we are programmed to live a certain way from the moment we are born.

I always did the "right" thing. I was a yes man, and a good little boy. I had followed the rules of the program step by step. If I did everything I was supposed to do, then why was I empty inside? Why did I feel like I was meant for so much more? Why was I longing to be more?

I didn't understand that I had been living in a program. Yes, I worked hard; I made every decision I needed to make. I sought to accomplish my goals. I was great at playing the game and following the rules. The problem? I had created my life within the program by default, following other people's ideas and standards without knowing what I wanted. I was living a life pleasing everyone and never asking the questions, "What does Jonathon want? How does Jonathon feel about this?" I made my decisions based on what I "should" do.

Some people are content in the program. I was one of those people. I wasn't aware there was a program until I was, and then there was no turning back.

Our environment shapes how we show up in this world. Our parents are the first programmers, modeling how to think and behave, unaware they too are programmed; and then we become programmed deeper by our siblings, friends, teachers, religion; and through TV, movies, music, commercials, politics, and through the rest of society.

We are placed in certain boxes, labeled as big, as small, black, white, brown, male, female, introvert, extrovert, gay, straight, good boy, bad girl, rich, poor, artistic, athletic, beautiful, ugly, college graduate, high school dropout, strong, weak, Christian, Muslim, Atheist, Democrat, Republican, realist, dreamer. The list goes on.

You become that label. You define what the acceptable behavior is from someone who lives within that stereotype. The more labels you add to your identity, the more you form a person with certain personality traits, insecurities, and how they live. It's fascinating to ponder the program and how we think we are different; yet we are the same, but with different labels on our boxes.

When you explore and realize how the program influences your life, you can create a new program. You become the driver. When you understand you can ultimately create the life you desire, you become the hero in your life. There is something inside whispering, guiding, protecting, and loving us along the way.

But are we aware of it?

Life has always worked out for me—that's a lie. It felt like there was more inside that I wouldn't allow to come out. I had so much untapped potential lying dormant below the surface. But hey, why rock the boat? I should be grateful.

Then I had my Moments of AHA!, moments of awakening. These are moments when you awaken to who you are and why you are here.

A Moment of AHA! is a powerful, expansive experience that feels good, such as getting married, having your first child, traveling the world, interacting with plant medicine (psychedelics), buying a home or landing your dream job.

Another way to experience Moments of AHA! is by having an experience that feels traumatic, such as getting a divorce, having a child before you think you are ready, the death of a loved one, a near-death experience, losing a job, or hitting rock bottom.

It could also be a simple moment in which someone said the right thing, at the right time, in the right way, for you to hear the message that could change your life. In those moments, you receive profound insights or epiphanies. Everything clicks.

CHAPTER 3
I'M TRIPPIN'

Allow me to take you back a few years before my world transformed. There was a build-up of many subtle Moments of AHA! that led me to my breakthrough. Some of these experiences were not so subtle, such as my profound and enlightening experiences with psilocybin, a naturally growing plant with healing potential, popularly known as magic mushrooms.

Psilocybin is a medicine that we should respect. Psilocybin, though natural and rare for people to overdose on it, is potent and can have life-altering effects, positive or negative.

I was hoping to have an intimate spiritual experience with my Creator. I was a devoted Christian, and I understood that there was potential to experience powerful insights, by using this medicine to connect with God on a deeper level.

If you're not familiar with psychedelics, it may sound like I was looking to lock myself away in my bedroom and trip my balls off. In some ways, you may be right.

I had taken mushrooms in the past with friends and usually had a significant experience. One time, I thought I was on the verge of death. It was one of the terrifying moments of my life, but the moment turned out to be one of the most intimate and loving experiences.

I thought it was a bad trip, but in reality I was experiencing a death of the ego. My ego was doing its best to control the experience, but I learned that control is not the approach with this medicine or life. That was a moment of AHA!

This medicine began as something of a curiosity. I had a close childhood friend, Michael, who had done it, and spoke highly of his experiences. He talked about how much he laughed, connected to music and nature, and discovered a deeper connection with friends.

Psilocybin can reveal the shadows that have been lurking in the corners of your soul. With great release comes great healing.

During that trip, I felt as if I was losing my mind, thinking that I was going crazy; and there were moments where I would go beyond paranoia, thinking that the cops were coming after us. These are all examples of having a bad trip. However, the medicine was releasing the negative energy subconsciously stored in my soul and in my body.

If we fight the medicine or attempt to control the experience of releasing these energies stored in the subconscious part of our bodies, then we will have a bad trip.

The medical field and science are on the leading edge of discovering the healing effects of this ancient medicine. So again, respect this medicine and all psychoactive plant medicines. There are safe ways in controlled environments where you can take part in healing ceremonies.

•

I was curious about the spiritual side of this medicine. The last time I took them, I thought I would die. I felt terrified to go on this journey alone and without a sounding board.

I presented the idea to my childhood friend Michael. I suggested we take the mushrooms separately at our own houses, and if things turned sketchy, we could meet up to help each other get into a better feeling space. Michael is fearless and full of life. He's the perfect person to share in these types of journeys. He stays grounded and confident, and creates a fun and safe place for others.

Our idea was to brew some mushroom tea at Michael's house, which was less than a mile away from my parent's home. We put our intentions into the tea, in how we would like the experience to go, and then I would head back to my house alone in my experience, while Michael would be alone in his.

We agreed that if one of us started tripping too hard, we would call each other and meet up. After a few hours, if all went well, we would meet up and finish the rest of the trip together.

At home, I headed to my room. I'm staring at this protein shaker bottle that's filled with brown and beige dirty-looking water and with the sediment of the mushrooms.

My palms are sweaty, my anxiety is through the roof, and I'm nervous about what's going to happen, as every psilocybin journey is different. I didn't know what to expect. This was my first time making the tea, and I heard it hits harder and much quicker this way, but you can ride the waves of the trip a tad easier.

I say, "Fuck it, cheers. Here we go. God, show yourself to me because I am an open vessel. I'm here, and I'm waiting. Let's talk. Let's meet. I'm ready. Bottoms up, Jonathon."

It tasted as disgusting as it looked. When I chugged that tea down, it tasted like mud, almost making me gag. But I felt happy, knowing that this natural mushroom from our Mother Earth will gift me with something extraordinary, and in gratitude, I savored the flavors of wet leaves, fresh soil, dry bark, and other earthy tones.

In under ten minutes, I had already felt the effects. If eaten as whole mushrooms, it usually takes close to 45 minutes to an hour to kick in. My anxiety increased, my breath got shallow, and I was feeling overwhelmed.

When you feel this way, sometimes it's good to hop into the shower and let the water cleanse you while also soothing the nerves to calm your body down. As I'm showering, I'm watching the water slide down my body, seeing every stream of liquid flowing so effortlessly, so free, so fluid. I perceived the streams of water as mini rivers playing through the crevices on my chest, then down to my toes. I started becoming one with the warmth and comfort of the water, as if something wrapped my whole body in a warm hug. The shower's heat was intensifying the effects of the mushrooms, and I laughed because I just got lost standing in my shower.

As the mushrooms started having more substantial effects, I thought that maybe this wasn't such a good idea. My mind goes into waves of doubt and enjoyment. "What the fuck was I thinking? What did I get myself into? Holy shit. I feel so fucking good. Damn, what is going on right now? Where am I?"

I laugh when I look back at the experience, as this is a normal part of the Psilocybin journey, which is why it's called a "trip." You go in and out of consciousness from the physical and energetic realms. There are waves, and you have to allow the waves to come and go, riding each one as they show up, just like the waves of everyday life.

When I got out of the shower, I lay down on my bed and listened to some music. I intended to listen to worship music, which was one of my favorite ways to connect to God. I went to church every week, and the music was what I considered most powerful.

The first song that I had listened to wasn't necessarily spiritual or worship music as I intended it, but it was a song that was recommended to me by a good friend. He said that next time I have a trip, I should watch this music video and listen to The Gorillaz song *Melancholy Hill*. You probably want to stop reading and watch the music video to understand how trippy it was. I watched that video five or six times in a row until I finally settled into the medicine.

Music has an immense influence when you are experiencing mushrooms because its vibration and frequency affects your energy. I have a specific playlist that loops when I do mushrooms, playing specific songs that uplift me and make me feel outstanding about myself and life. I call it, "The Happiest Trip."

At any point, when I need a reminder of how amazing I am as a human being, or just a little pick me up, I turn on this playlist. It helps me not only when I'm using psilocybin, but any time in my everyday grind, when I'm feeling a little off. It will instantly center me. The more I listen to these songs, the more they are bringing me up to my highest self.

After listening to the song a handful of times, my anxiety had dissipated. I felt as if I had melted into my bed. I enjoyed how wonderful my body felt while having the biggest smile imprinted on my face from ear to ear. Tears fell over my cheeks. It was time to listen to some worship music. I closed my eyes and just soaked in every note and the beautiful melodies of the acoustic guitars, the serenity of the piano, and every prayer expressed by those artists. I felt as if I was embracing the wholeness and magnitude of our Creator.

I was praising the God of Gods, the Highest of High, the Alpha and Omega, and the omnipresent God that moves the mountain, calms the seas, and places the infinite stars in the sky.

Take a moment and let that sink in. Whether you think it to be authentic doesn't matter. Feel what an energy or entity of that great magnitude feels like if it were true. Feel what it does to your body, your mind, and your soul. It's expansive, supportive, intimate, and loving.

I listened to an assortment of songs and felt as if my mind was stretched and pulled apart, thinking about how truly grand and extraordinary it was to exist.

I never thought about the expansiveness of our universe. I went on a visual journey, leading to a zoomed-out perspective of being above our earth, seeing all of its parts. I could look at each of the planets of our solar system, travel to witness the star we rotate around, the sun; and notice the perfect distance the earth is from this star. I saw how consistent it revolves while understanding its perfect proximity to the other planets and their never-ending rotation.

From there, I zoomed out further, observing the 100 billion suns in our single galaxy, the Milky Way. I went further to see the 100 billion galaxies that each hold 100 billion stars, stars that make our sun look like a grain of sand.

After that, I returned to earth. I realized that this planet that we live on isn't even part of the count of those 100 billion stars in our galaxy. We are a spec of a planet, capable of fitting 1.3 million earths into our sun, a grain of sand compared to other suns, and our planet floats around that grain of sand.

I zoomed in further to recognize that we were sticking to this planet by an unseen force called gravity. We don't float away, no; we stay connected and grounded to what we call home. I am one of almost eight billion humans. I zoomed in more to view the variety of plants, flowers, animals, and bugs in this world. I went deeper and observed the sands of our beaches, the forests, the rivers, the unfamiliar landscapes, and the extreme contrasts of weather. I saw the evolution of our creation. I saw all that we had invented, built, and expanded on while living here.

I zoomed in deeper still, viewing each cell of my body, every molecule, and felt the miracle of how my body works and functions with no conscious effort on my part. At this moment, time disappeared. I saw the perfection of how I got to this point in space. I witnessed my ancestors aligning with one another through synchronicities and magic to create life and families through generation after generation, leading to my existence, the 300,000 eggs within my grandmother's womb, connecting with the exact sperm to create life. The luck that it took for the previous lineage to meet and stay together so that I can be here. We exist despite everything working against us. Maybe the universe isn't working against us, but working for us?

The depth of this experience gave me perspective and understanding of what I am. I realized God was not some old white guy with a long beard. God was a force of creation, a force of energy, a force of expansion and love. I had put God in a box my entire life, and now that box was removed. God is the energy that binds all that exists from an atomic photon to the galaxies light-years away, yet he is still creating and expanding. This energy is beginningless and endless. At that moment, I had the revelation that the God I knew was not the God of the Universe.

Perhaps God doesn't judge us, or is jealous of us, or condemns us to some eternal hell if we don't follow the rules or laws of a certain book. God is much more infinite and unconditional than I could ever conceive. These emotions that I thought God had were human, and I now know that God is much more beyond a human's conditional mind. If we understood what this Force of creation is, our brain would most likely break.

I understand this could be the mushrooms speaking, but that was my intention with this experience. It wanted to share in an intimate space with the Creator of all that was, all that is, and all that will ever be. Sharing in the intimacy of that space became the most personal experience I had ever had, and it shaped how I saw the world and everything in it.

When I jumped out of bed, I took a fresh look at the world through the bedroom window. I wanted to make sure I wasn't dreaming or losing my mind; that I was still living in a physical reality. It felt as if I had left this dimension, for an expedition to find the answers to the universe. When I looked out of my window, for the first time perhaps, I saw life across the street. It had always been there, yet I had never seen it.

It came as a giant, beautiful tree, living underneath a light post that perfectly illuminated its vibrancy; it was alive and breathing. I could see it expanding and contracting as it was dancing in the wind. I could see the vibrational energy field that was within the tree and that surrounded the tree. We looked at each other as we both saw each other for the first time. I laughed as I felt as if the tree was playing with me. It was such a surreal and magical moment. Again, it could have been because of the magic mushrooms. But the more I connected with the tree, the more I was giggling. The more I laughed, the funnier it became. I was aware of how ridiculous it was, laughing at a tree as I'm peaking out of my bedroom window, tripping my balls off on some magic mushrooms, which made it even more hilarious. I laughed until I cried, and then laughed more until my abs cramp up, my cheeks hurt, and I laughed until I couldn't laugh any longer. How beautiful laughter is for the soul. That was such a healing moment for me.

Within the next 30 minutes following that silly experience with that tree, Michael and I met up at the park down the street. It was pitch black. The lights were off, but we didn't care. I brought my basketball so that we could shoot the ball around. We were both outstanding athletes, and we were pretty competitive when we played against each other in sports. We played a game of 21.

This game lasted forever, but it could have been 20 minutes, as time is hard to keep track of when on psilocybin. Late-night sprinklers had soaked the ground. It felt like we weren't on a basketball court but on a slip 'n' slide. We could hardly make a shot, but we had so much fun. We could barely breathe because we were laughing so hard. It felt as though we were just kids on a basketball court for the first time, discovering this beautiful sport that we both loved, and were there for the fun of the game.

Michael and I spent the next few hours laughing and reflecting on the epiphanies we received. We had a solo journey, but we were never alone. We talked about how the little things that we usually worry about in life didn't matter. Those things don't matter as much as we thought they did. What does matter is how we treat other people. What does matter is how we decide to show up every day. We talked about how we could indeed be an example in this world, by breaking open our potential and transferring it to the surrounding people.

That conversation was one where I placed a bookmark in my book of life. I still come back to that moment, as it was a profound conversation and exchange of energy I had with my friend. That night shifted my perspective on life, and about people, and about God. I made some changes in my life after that, but nothing too dramatic. I still lived in my box, but I upgraded to a box with a little more space.

CHAPTER 4
I Cracked

On the day my soul cracked, I learned my mom had a tumor in her brain.

I've always had a fantastic relationship with my mom. She was someone I looked up to as one of my spiritual guides, the one I spoke with about God, read the Bible with, and went to church with every week. My mom has been one of my best friends. I never talked to my mom about my psychedelic experience until now. I was afraid of how she might view it or me.

We are eating at Baja Fresh, a tiny Mexican Cantina. We talked about God and how amazing He is, and the love Jesus had for us. You know, all that fun Christian talk. I decided lunch was a perfect time for me to open up about the psychedelic experience, and how I viewed God and how I went into that space, intending to connect with our Creator.

I told her how I had placed God in a box my whole life, and perhaps I had my image of God all wrong. I further explained my new perspective, and how I understood God is beyond anything that I could ever fathom with my human mind.

My mom is a loving person, considerate and accepting of all people, yet I was still anxious about how she would react, learning that her baby boy sometimes likes to trip on magic mushrooms. I should have given my mom more credit; she was understanding. We continued talking about The God of The Universe. The moment was so present, so raw, and I felt as if I was vibrating while speaking about the profoundness of our shared viewpoint of spirituality.

We were reaching the end of our lunch when the conversation took a turn. Mom began by telling me everything was okay and there's no need to worry. When someone tells you that there is nothing to worry about, you worry.

She continued to tell me she's been going through a tough time, and she has had to deal with it privately. The only people that knew about this were my oldest sister and my father. She reassured me that everything would be okay and this all-loving, all-knowing, and all-powerful God would take care of her. He is healing, and we are in His hands. Everything is always working out for a bigger reason, and He sends His angels here to comfort us and protect us when we most need them.

I was feeling more concerned.

I told her, "I know, mom. God has always been there for our family. But what's going on? Is everything okay?"

She told me she received some scans back from her doctor that revealed a golf ball size tumor in her head, and that the tumor was benign so there was no cancer, yet she had a decent size growth in her brain that needed a check-up every six months. She could choose to either get the tumor removed or live with it. Her choice? To live with it! She expressed her confidence and strength through scripture, as she always did, "Do not fear, for I Am with you."

The news rocked me, but I took a deep breath and put on a solid face with my usual smile, like I had done my whole life for my family, mom, sisters, and everyone else. It displayed my confidence that everything would be just fine, that I wasn't hurting. I'm strong. I'm firm.

But it was all a lie. It was a mask.

After lunch, we hugged, embracing longer than usual, and then left.

As soon as I got into my car, my mask came off. As soon as I sat down, I let it out. I had an overwhelming amount of pain and fear of losing my mom, friend, spiritual guide, and the person who loves me more than anyone else in this world. I sat there for 20 minutes sobbing. I don't think I have ever cried so intensely, previous to that moment. It was the first time that I had ever thought about my parent's time here being so limited. They would not be here forever. I cried not just for my mom, but also for my dad, sisters, and friends. We are so fragile. Life is so short. We could go at any moment.

Although I felt afraid that my mom would have to live with a brain tumor, I felt grateful that it wasn't cancer. I said a prayer, accepting what was happening and that it was part of life. My mom is one of the strongest people I know. Little did I know that that moment was only trying to open me up for what was to come. I had cracked something inside of me that would soon break open.

CHAPTER 5
I'M BROKEN

One month later, I woke up to a missed call from Vicky, Michael's sister. Her call was out of the ordinary. I called her back. Before she answered, my mind was jetting to all the plausible reasons she would be calling. I was thinking maybe Michael got pulled over last night after partying and issued a DUI? Perhaps he was in a car accident? Perhaps Vicky was planning something nice for her little brother. My mind was racing. Why is she contacting me?

After a few rings, she picked up. "Dugan?"

"Hey Vicky. What's going on? Is everything okay?"

"Michael's dead. Michael died last night."

In disbelief, I stuttered, "Wha... wha... what do you mean? What are you talking about?"

"Michael died last night, Dugan. He didn't wake up. His heart stopped. He's dead."

Tears welled up in my eyes. I took a breath and asked what she and her family needed.

"We are at his apartment. We would really like it if you came to be with us."

I let her know I was on my way.

As soon as I got off the phone, I dropped to my knees. My chest tightened. I couldn't catch my breath. My brain couldn't comprehend that Michael, my best friend since I was seven, was dead—poof, disappeared from this physical world. And now I'm preparing to go to his apartment for the last time and say goodbye for the last time, to see the shell of his body.

I struggled to my feet and went upstairs to wake up my wife. My wife, myself and Michael had all worked together for the last few years at the same restaurant. When I tried to get the words out nothing came. I started sobbing hysterically. I remember the look of horror on my wife's face. She jumped out of bed.

"Oh my gosh, what happened? What happened, Jonathon? No. No. No. Tell me what happened? Take a breath, Jonathon? I'm here."

"It's Michael. Michael died last night."

She grabbed and held me so tight. I was crying in her arms, and she repeated, "I'm so sorry. I love you. I'm so sorry."

After a few minutes, I pulled myself together. "It's time for me to leave and be with Michael's family."

That moment with my wife was one of the first times that I had ever allowed someone else to be there for me. I had always been someone who didn't cry or show emotion, but would rather shove them deep, deep down, where I hoped I would never have to experience them again.

That worked for only so long. I was like a bottle of soda that was shaken up, on the verge of an explosion. Michael's dying was breaking me open. What I had shoved deep down was now going to surface and present itself over the next few months.

•

I spent that day with Michael's family. I met his girlfriend, who he had been dating for about a year. Michael would always tell me how much he loved her. Yet this was our first meeting because I never took time to make meeting her a priority. I thought there was more time.

I would tell him, "We can meet the next time we do something together, I promise."

We never know if there is a next time. This time, there wasn't. I had to meet Michael's girlfriend on the day he left this world.

Michael's family, broken and devastated, were sitting in the lobby of his small apartment complex. I remember the vibrant orange, red, and green colors, a modern and hip style. While I waited in the lobby to go upstairs to Michael's apartment, I remember hearing the song *Photograph* by Ed Sheeran playing over a radio.

I remember how I felt standing in the elevator. I was breaking. There was a metallic scent with stale air. On the fourth floor, the hallway was dark and closing in, squeezing me tight as I moved toward Michael's apartment.

Michael was lying there, lifeless, no longer an energetic, laughing, and loving person I knew. He was just a shell. His family and I gathered around him, held his hands, kissed him, prayed, and then one-by-one said our goodbyes.

It was a painful experience. I just observed Michael's family, feeling their heartbreak, sharing my heartbreak, and witnessing his girlfriend's brokenness. I had barely spoken. My chest felt like it was going to rupture, my tongue stuck to the roof of my mouth, and my jaw clamped tight. I stared blankly. I hardly shed any tears. I was doing my best to hold on to everything. I was in shock.

•

Every memory that Michael and I had shared was flooding my mind. I remember the first time we connected during my fourth-grade birthday party. It pissed me off that another friend had invited him. I thought he was a jerk and a bully. But I learned he was kind. We laughed and played water basketball in the pool, and I realized he liked to talk shit, and he was highly competitive.

I had him all wrong. He was like me. I was also a shit talker that was all about winning. We stayed friends as we both made each other better. I remember the moments we skateboarded together, the summer when, as freshman football players, we had almost a perfect season and then, just a year later, driving home from Reno with a state championship.

We would get into fights, wrestle, jump on the trampoline, and laugh a lot. We worked at JCPenney together for the Christmas season, carpooling, smoking a blunt after work, and then watching *The Voice*, an Acapella singing show.

On my wedding day, he stood next to me. At the end of that night, he disappeared for 30 minutes. We were curious where he had gone, but this wasn't out of the ordinary for him to vanish in the middle of the night. But he came back this time with bags from Taco Bell. There were 14 people at our wedding party, and when everyone saw Michael walking up with the healing food after a long day of drinking and smoking, they filled up with overwhelming joy. He was their hero, and they were cheering him on.

That may not seem like such a profound moment, but that's how Michael lived—moments at a time. He brought so much joy to every room. Those little moments created tremendous impacts.

I reflected on our magic mushroom trips. He helped me through the time I had the bad trip; where I thought I was about to die, along with sharing my best trip with him. We took this healing medicine multiple times together, exchanging energy, talking about life, and how we wanted to change the world. We pondered how to be better humans, stress less, and love more by the way we show up in the world.

Some of these memories hurt, giving me a deep sense of loss. Other memories filled me up with immense gratitude and laughter. I was one lucky guy to have known such a lively and vibrant human being. He is the reason I am the man I am today. He woke me the fuck up out of my slumber.

On a high school football field, on the same grounds as our graduation ceremony years before, and at Michael's funeral, I spoke about my best friend. Public speaking was not my forte. Speaking in public terrified me, but this time I felt different.

I didn't worry about how I looked or if anyone would judge me. I was honoring Michael and his family. He made a difference in many people's lives. If I didn't speak about the value that he gave me while he was on this earth, my future self would live in regret.

At Michael's funeral I spoke in front of hundreds of people. I didn't understand what was transforming inside me when I declared how I planned to live a fuller life because of my friend's example. I explained how Michael's death has awakened me.

I told them about my realizations in the days following Michael's death. If I was to trade places, and I was the one who died instead, would I be proud of how I lived? Would I be satisfied with my legacy? Did I live my life full out and strive to maximize my potential? My answer to those questions was an absolute no. I had been playing it safe all my life. I didn't want to rock the boat. I was living a good life, but I wasn't actualizing my potential. I was afraid to look.

"Michael didn't show me I was afraid of death, but showed me I was afraid of dying before I lived. He taught me it's not about how long or wide you live, but how deep you live."

I continued to tell everyone that our lives are so fragile, and that Michael showed us we could die in an instant. So what type of life have we been living? What have we been taking for granted? Or are we asleep? It's time to wake up because we won't be here forever. We have all heard that all it takes is one person to change the world. I never believed it. I wanted to believe in that saying, but I didn't think that it was possible.

Michael changed that for me. One person can change the world. Maybe he didn't change the world for the 8 billion people on this earth, but he changed the world of at least one person. He changed my world.

I now understand that changing the world is about how deeply you can change the lives of others. If Michael could change my life, then maybe I can too? Maybe you can?

"Be the change you wish to see in the world."

Michael understood. It's time for us to embrace this belief and know that now it's our turn to change the world, beginning with us.

•

This is when I learned of CT Fletcher. I had the honor of reading a letter Vicky had written on behalf of their family during a candlelight service. The letter finished with, "It's Still Your Mother Fucking Set."

I asked Vicky what that meant.

"Dugan, you don't know who CT Fletcher is? What the hell?" She told me who he was and why he was important to Michael. Michael faithfully wore a rubber bracelet on both wrists, one that held CT's catchphrase, "Fuck Excuses," and the other, "ISYMFS."

Fletcher was a world champion weightlifter. He worked his ass off to become an elite athlete. He now coaches other weightlifters to become world champions. When you think about the concept, "It's

Still Your Mother Fucking Set," you might link it to lifting weights. You are at the gym doing set after set, and yet you are never done.

That makes sense and applies to weightlifting or any sport, but it goes deeper. What happens when life gets hard and you feel like quitting? "It's Still Your Mother Fucking Set!" What happens when you don't feel like going to work, but the rent is due? "It's Still Your Mother Fucking Set!" What happens when you face loss and defeat in your business? "It's Still Your Mother Fucking Set!" What happens when you work overtime, and your spouse and children are looking to spend time with you? "It's Still Your Mother Fucking Set!"

What happens when someone you love dies? We don't have the luxury to give up in life and hope that everything works out. Life is a process. The only thing that exists is a process, the journey, and the path to that never-ending destination. It's never-ending because when we arrive at the perceived destination, it's satisfying for a moment, but then we move the finish line for ourselves by creating a new destination.

We are ever-expanding and ever-evolving beings. In reality, there is no finish line. That means, "It's Still Your Mother Fucking Set!" Don't stop, keep going, keep moving, hold your head up high. You got this. You are stronger and greater than you even know.

"It's Still Your Mother Fucking Set!"

It doesn't matter how tired you are, how sick you are, or how many hardships you face, your set never finishes. You have another one inside. It's ready, waiting, so you can grow to be stronger, grow emotionally, and teach others how you have overcome your challenges through your example.

Decide where this analogy fits in your own life. Just because my best friend died doesn't mean that I get to make excuses and give up. I felt as if I must start living life for two people now. Anytime I'm in an uncomfortable position, where I feel nervous, scared, or tired, I think of how my best friend isn't here to feel these emotions, but if he were, I bet he would say, "It's Still Your Mother Fucking Set!"

And keep moving forward by transmuting those emotions into strength, because that's the type of person he was. Nothing would stop Michael. Feeling a deep sense of pain helped me experience the connectivity and expansion of love. The heaviness of death taught me the lightness of life. The mundaneness of sleepwalking through life has shown me how exciting it is to be awake. The fleeting happiness you feel achieving a materialist goal, can allow you to understand the lasting fulfillment of having a purpose. Falling and failure educate us in learning how to stand back up and succeed.

We must face the dark corners of our consciousness and soul to allow our light to shine on those who need us the most. I asked a sequence of essential questions after Michael died. "If I died, instead of him, would I be satisfied with the life that I had lived? What kind of legacy would I have left behind? Do I feel like I lived up to my potential? If I died today, would I be proud of the person I was?" If I was honest, I still had so much to give to myself and to the world.

For the next six months I repeated to myself, "It's Still Your Mother Fucking Set!" I didn't feel strong in my life. I'm still unsure why or in what ways Michael's death affected me so profoundly, but I cried almost every day for six months. I am the type of person who doesn't show that type of emotion. It's weak, it's embarrassing, and it's not manly. Or at least that was my old self speaking to me.

For the first time in my life, I would say I experienced depression, anxiety, anger, fear, and went down a spiral of isolation. It fucked me up. I felt that everything I was experiencing had been trapped inside me for years, and it now had space to be released. These were the parts I had shoved deep inside, where I thought they would be locked down forever.

Michael's death broke me open to the extent where my past wounds spewed out. For the next few months after his death, I experienced more than pain and hurt. I would start crying in the littlest moments. Whenever I saw a butterfly or ladybug, tears would stream down my face. I would see a blooming flower, and I would choke up. Every time I looked into the eyes of a friend or one of my family members, I beamed with the overwhelming emotion of love. I experienced my emotions. I didn't hold back because of any preconceived judgments of what was worthy of "good" or "bad" emotions—all emotion is part of the human experience. If I block the ones that hurt, I plug the ones that feel good.

As uncomfortable as I felt, it was the most alive I felt.

I knew that my life had to change. I knew I must become more. I must live up to my potential. But I didn't know how to move forward. I didn't know what I was moving toward.

What did I know?

"It Was Still My Mother Fucking Set!"

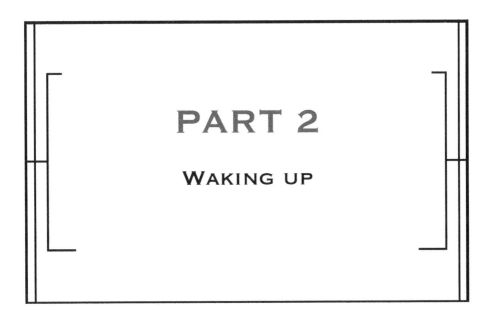

PART 2

WAKING UP

CHAPTER 6
I'M LISTENING

During this period, when I'm open, feeling, and listening to the whispers of life, I discovered a multitude of tools to help align with my inner voice, such as journaling, reading, listening to audiobooks, podcasts, hiking, yoga, and meditation.

Meditation was the first of these tools, which I believe was the seed that led to these other life-changing tools. I believed meditation was something that made you feel relaxed and focused. I didn't know what it was, because I had never experienced how it made you feel; or did any research on the benefits of meditation; nor did I have any interest until this time in my life.

Growing up as a Christian, I resisted meditation and yoga and was told that those practices are of other religions and it was a worship of their Gods. So, to a devoted Christian, you can see how it was something I wasn't looking to tap into, out of fear and ignorance. Fortunately, in this broken place, I was listening to what life offered. I was open to trying new things.

A few months after Michael passed away, I met up with another of our best friends and Michael's girlfriend. We went to Michael's favorite park, which was full of trees and animals. You don't get that too often in Vegas. Michael spent a lot of his time here, so we thought it was a good place to catch up, to see how we were all doing, and smoke a blunt since this was something we often partook in with Michael. It was an extremely cold night in the Northside of Las Vegas, perhaps not cold for others in the world, but I would consider this night to be bone chilling. It was a windy evening and the sun had dropped, and I thought it was a good idea to wear basketball shorts in mid-November. I've definitely had better ideas.

My friend Bobby rolled a blunt for us. Michael always thought the communion of this medicine was part healing and part art. When you're rolling a blunt, you use all of your senses. You visually see the vibrant colors of the flower, primarily green, but some have purple in them, with bright orange and golden hairs and tiny white fuzzy crystals. When you break the weed apart with your fingers, the fragrance disperses sweet, earthy and fruity notes into the air. Then your fingers get sticky and filled with dust particles of this ancient flower, and you lick them. After breaking open the bud, you pack the tobacco paper full, softly and gently roll it in a perfect cylinder, lick the meeting points to bind this beautiful blunt to share with the people you love. I couldn't agree with Michael more that the process of blunt-rolling is also healing and art.

As we enjoyed smoking the blunt, we reminisced about some memories we had experienced with Michael. We talked about dealing with our loss and offered each other words of hope and encouragement. I was loving our conversations, but I get cold when I smoke weed. I get fucking cold, freezing to where my whole body is uncontrollably shaking. My teeth were chattering, and I could barely get a complete sentence out while I'm telling a story. It was halfway funny and halfway embarrassing.

Bobby asked me if I had ever meditated before. I responded with a quick, "Yes, of course. I work out consistently, pray every day, and love to zone out to music. Those would be my forms of meditation." Bobby, the kind soul that he is, politely answered, "Cool, Jon, those are all amazing tools that help you relax. I'm curious, though, have you ever done any traditional meditation or breathwork?"

I told him, "Well, no, but I'm definitely open to trying it if you wouldn't mind leading it?"

With a big smile on Bobby's face, "I'd love that." Sitting on a log bench, Bobby guided us in my first meditation alongside Heidy, Michael's girlfriend. "I'll make it really simple, you guys. Sit in a position where you feel comfortable, rest your hands in your lap, straighten your back, and look within by closing your eyes. From there, we are just going to take a breath in through your nose for, let's say, four to five seconds, then you will breathe out through your mouth for the same time that you breathed in, and that's it. Keep your focus by counting your breath. Let's begin. Breathe in through your nose, 1-2-3-4-5 and exhale through your mouth, 1-2-3-4-5. Repeat until you feel you're done. Any questions?"

Heidy and I looked at each other, and we both felt like we were ready to dive right in.

We meditated. My mind was all over the place, and I was miserably cold as my body shook. I continued to remind myself of Bobby's instructions, "Focus on counting your breath." So I kept counting, 1-2-3-4-5 and exhale 1-2-3-4-5 inhale 1-2-3-4-5 exhale 1-2-3-4-5."

After a few rounds of this, my mind was quiet, and everything around me was disappearing. I felt as if I was disappearing. Before I knew it, I felt warm. I was no longer shivering, and it comfortably melted me into my seat. Time didn't exist at this moment. I was completely present. My chest felt like it was wide open, and overwhelmed with gratitude for my friends, and for how Michael had brought us together.

The surrounding sounds intensified, and it seemed as if someone was playing a song right above my head with a maraca shaker, knowing that it was just the wind ruffling through the leaves of the surrounding trees. The cool crisp air kissed my cheeks, and tears ran down my face. I had an overwhelming smile from ear to ear. The top of my head was warm and tingly, and I had this interesting feeling as if I had arrived. Where did I arrive, you wonder? Home—I felt as if I had finally made it home. Love engulfed me. It was such a beautiful and serene moment that changed my life. This was another one of those Moments of AHA!

We opened our eyes simultaneously with no words needing to be spoken, as if we understood it was time to move on. I thought my eyes were closed for just a few minutes, but Bobby told us we were sitting there for 15 minutes. I couldn't believe it. Time had disappeared. We shared our experiences together before calling it a night.

I can't express enough how grateful I am to Bobby for introducing me to meditation on that cold night. This is where my healing journey began.

•

Over the next few months, I became obsessed with practicing meditation. It silenced the outside noise and allowed me to be abundantly aware of what was happening inside. Meditation assisted me in processing my emotions, understanding my thoughts and brought in a new relationship with myself and others.

I also began practising journaling. I felt like it was vital for me to write what I was experiencing in these meditations, and hoped that it would help me process them.

I learned about all forms of meditation, and I dove into as many as I could. They all gave me distinct sensations inside my body, within my mind, and throughout my energy field. I honestly don't think I would have used the phrase "energy field" before meditating because I hadn't experienced it before that time. The more I meditated, the deeper it took me into different parts of my body, releasing traumatic memories, then helping me forgive and heal them. My mind went quieter the deeper I went, showing me different visions of my friend Michael visiting me, God visiting me, and angels visiting me. The more silence I was experiencing, a whisper crept in and spoke to me. This whisper was a familiar whisper, one that I had known my whole life. I had been praying and talking to this voice since I was a boy, but I had never gotten quiet enough to listen to what it had to say back to me.

This voice was my saving grace. It felt like I was healing daily. I would be in a meditation one day and come out of it sobbing, as it brought me back to a childhood experience where I had felt immense pain. During another session, I would laugh so hard that I couldn't breathe, which also brought me into tears, but not from pain. It was from ecstasy. The ecstasy of overwhelming joy and love fully aligned and embodied with the oneness of The Creator who made me, the life that I was living, and everything that existed around me. For the first time in my life, I shut the fuck up and listened.

The six months following Michael's death had been the most expansive and growth-oriented time of my life. I questioned everything about life; I never questioned it before, as I didn't feel like it was necessary. Why question the things that I was told to believe? It's been working for me so far. It's been working for my parents and their parents, so I'll just be a good little boy and follow the path.

The way I was living life was not working. I asked all of those existential questions of who, what, when, where, and why about my life, about God, purpose, religion, relationships with friends, family, my wife, and existence. Why are we here if we come to live and die? What's the point? Who is God, what is God, and how does God work? Who is Jesus? Why do we have to go through Him to get to The Ultimate Source of All That Is? Shouldn't we have a direct line? I forbade myself to even think about these questions, believing that it was blasphemy, but I needed to understand. I knew God would provide the answers if I stayed receptive.

As the months went by, the more that whisper answered these questions, along with answering questions I didn't even know that I had. The voice either gave me direct answers during meditation or guided me towards different ancient texts, podcasts, audible books, or articles online. Sometimes my answers would come during my journaling sessions. I would write to a stream of consciousness, where it felt like words were channeling onto the paper in ways that I had never written before. Memories that I had never recalled would show up in my writing.

Outside of meditation and journaling, I hiked in nature. It was something Michael was into, so I thought I would try it. Maybe I would feel his presence more out there. Hiking was definitely out of my comfort zone. When I was growing up, I absolutely hated hiking. I didn't understand why anyone enjoyed it. I was extremely competitive, being an athlete, and obsessed with the destination as if it were the finish line, and I victoriously conquered the mountain.

Every time I arrived at a destination, I felt underwhelmed. I would say, "This looks just like the rest of the hike. It all looks the same. What's so great about the destination?"

I didn't realize how much truth I was speaking in my younger years, but my perception of it was off. Hiking is a direct mirror of life. There is nothing more special about the destination, as it is short-lived and fleeting. The path to get there holds as much beauty and value all along the way. That's where we spend most of our time. The journey is what it's all about, and when we can fully embrace and enjoy the journey, the destination will taste that much more delicious.

I fell in love with hiking after a friend took me to a few of his favorite spots. I realized how much value nature had for me. I would hike alone three to four times a week at Red Rock Canyon. During my hikes I would listen to an audible book or to music, and set a timer every 10 to 15 minutes to do a one-minute meditation to remind myself to pay attention to the surrounding beauty.

This was important for me because I don't know about you, but there have been many times when I hiked I realized I hadn't looked up the entire time, until I had accomplished getting to the destination. Again, it's another metaphor for life and how I once lived. I would accomplish so many things and miss out on every step that led me to that accomplishment. If we aren't looking up, then life is going to pass us by. There is always beauty available if we are aware enough to adjust the lens we look through. It might come naturally for some people to view the world in this way, but it took practice and a lot for me. I took this practice to the next level and set timers throughout my day. When it went off, no matter what I was doing or where I was at, I would find a moment to close my eyes, take a deep breath, reset, open my eyes, and find any bit of beauty that I could hook on to around me. I would express gratitude for the experience of that moment. It's a powerful exercise to practice for more presence.

Going back to hiking, when I would get to the top of the route, I would spend 15 to 20 minutes meditating on the sounds and energy of nature. Ralph Waldo Emerson once said, "Let us be silent, that we may hear the whispers of the Gods." I couldn't agree more. The whisper spoke louder in nature. I connected more to my writing in nature. I felt as if I retained more of the information from the books when I was in nature, and I thought that every time I was in nature, my soul healed more and more. In nature, we find answers to most questions.

After every hike, I felt more alive and lighter. It felt as if I hiked to the top of the mountain with a backpack of boulders, and when I got to the top, I could remove a boulder which lightened my load. This backpack of overbearing weight is something we all carry. We have carried it since we were children, and finally, I could release some of this weight.

I felt that I might have been going a little crazy during this time of my life. I saw visions while hearing the whisper in my head, feeling as if nature were healing me. I was locking myself in my room with my eyes closed, breathing deeply, and I was crying almost every day— alone, confused, and felt as if everything in life was a lie. Wouldn't you feel crazy?

•

I know my intuition guided me to these tools, leading to my realizations. I can't explain it better than I was being guided; again, crazy right? What's more interesting, is that I was being guided to a variety of places to find my answers.

I discovered the benefits and science behind these tools. I learned that spending a minimum of ten minutes in nature could reduce your heart rate, lower your anxiety, assist with creativity, and heal trauma. Meditation can bring you from a sympathetic state, fight or flight, to a parasympathetic state, rest and digest. Another way to say it is meditation can get you to a mental state where you experience different brain waves. It can take you from beta, a faster wavelength, alert and externally focused, to alpha, a slightly slower wavelength, which is more internal, calm, and creative. You can go even deeper into a slower brain wave called theta. This is a deep state of bliss, feeling fully connected. Time disappears, visions come to life, and healing occurs. Some go into the delta, a state of deep sleep and gamma experienced through channeling.

Journaling helps bring awareness and understanding about your thoughts and emotions, while helping you process events and desires by finding clarity. A study at the Dominican University in California reports that you are 42% more likely to achieve your goals if you consistently write them down, as you activate both of the hemispheres of your brain. You can remember events in more detail if you journal about them, more than you would by looking at a picture. An overwhelming amount of studies prove the abundance of healing and benefits these tools bring to one's life.

We decide what works best for us, and I present these tools to you. They have worked for me and many other influencers in history. Then they can also work for you if you are open to them and consistently practice.

It's about time to switch shit up and get out of your comfort zone. If you don't change what you do, then nothing will change. If life is going great for you right now, I'm happy for you. I pray for even more joy, love, and blessings, but what if there were more levels to how great your life could be? What if what you think is a level 10 happiness is only a level five? Our scales of measurements are so subjective. We only know what we know, and there are levels to everything. I encourage you to continue to ask for more, strive for more, be eager for more, and yet be grateful for where you are at in the perfection of what you are as a human being. Where you are now is taking you to where you are going. Love this version of yourself, your past version, and the future version. They are YOU. You receive all that you desire, but you can't wait for anyone to give it to you. You must decide to take this opportunity to become more connected to the inner YOU.

CHAPTER 7
THE TRANSFORMATION

We all have questions about how the universe works. I encourage everyone to question. Curiosity with the openness to learn and understand is where expansion is born. I'm a firm believer that the universe wants to give us what we want, whether it's answers to a question or requesting a physical manifestation. The universe will bring it into our experience if we are able, open, ready, and willing.

I won't go through all the answers received from my questions. Most people have these questions but aren't always willing to admit it to themselves or others. I felt a sense of shame asking certain questions, or felt people were judging me as I judged myself. Sometimes I thought some questions didn't have an answer, or I would feel insignificant or unworthy asking specific questions. Sometimes I felt God would judge me.

Then I learned there is an answer to every question. Again, if there is a question, there is an answer—always. I discovered God does not judge us; we judge us. Our judgement towards others reflects on us, and in return, we judge ourselves. It's normal to be curious, and curiosity is how we grow into new spaces of understanding.

The last few reasons, and maybe there's more; but there were also times when I didn't want to ask a question, because if you ask there is a possibility that you may get the answer, and with that answer you must take responsibility for that new basis of knowledge. Who wants to do that when ignorance is bliss? Why would I want to try something new? I lived a life full of excuses, full of fear of failing, and I felt content living in the comfort of my box. When I could move through all the bullshit excuses of being a dimmed version of who I was, things quickly shifted.

As every movie breaks into scenes, every book into chapters, and every year by seasons, life breaks into phases. This phase of my life was about breaking down what I thought I knew about who I was, who God was, and about the meaning of life. I was recreating the foundation of my core beliefs, how I thought, and the actions I took daily to redirect the future of my life and actualize the potential that had been dormant. This is where my transformation took place.

How I like to define transformation is a process of experiences that takes you from one form of being to another. To experience a positive transformation, you must tap into your inner potential and then execute. Everyone has potential, but we also have a limitless and never ending potential.

How do you actualize your potential? How do you take what's inside you and bring it out into the world for all to see? This is a question that every leader has asked since the beginning of time. I will not claim that I have the answer that trumps over all other philosophies and methods of leading others to actualize potential, but I believe if you experience what I'm about to tell you, then it's inevitable that after time, you will live a more full life, a life created by you, and no one else—a life where you are more joyful, empowered, and alive. It's a life where you experience love, connection, and meaning. You can have an abundant life, full of blessings and laughter. It might not happen overnight and there might be some darker days than others, but I promise that if you stay open and take it one step at a time, then you will get glimpses of this life I speak of more and more, until eventually and habitually it's experienced consistently. The sun WILL rise to a miraculous and beautiful day.

I believe there are four key components that if you OWN them and you experience them consistently, then you will actualize your potential:

1. Opening your mind

2. Connecting to your heart

3. Awakening your soul

4. Aligning your behavior

Before I go into more detail about each of these components, you must understand no one can tap into YOUR potential, as it ultimately belongs to you, and only you. You must OWN YOUR REALITY. Your existence belongs to you, and it's nobody's responsibility to create your life. That responsibility is yours, so if you want to improve your life, it's time to stop waiting. No more looking around to see if anyone is going to come to your rescue. No more making excuses why life is hard and isn't working out for you. It doesn't matter if every excuse that you spit out is valid, because the fucked up thing about excuses is that most are valid. They are REAL. It might be true that your life is harder than that person over there, but NOW WHAT? What are you going to do about it? You can drown in sorrow, self-pity, bitterness, and anger your whole life, wishing things coulda, woulda, or shoulda been different, but they are not. It might be hard at first to admit that the reason your life is the way it is right now is YOUR FAULT, but eventually it gets easier. Not only does it get easier but also you will feel empowered that you have all the control to redirect your life. Whether life is going great for you right now or not doesn't matter. It feels amazing to know that you can adjust the areas that need adjusting in order for you to get results. If you don't take ownership of your life, then you will always be at the mercy of how life wants to mold you, rather than you molding life to how you would like to experience it.

Now that you are ready to own your reality, here is the first component of actualizing potential.

1. Opening Your Mind

The older we get, the more fixed the hard drive of our mind gets. Not that it can't be changed and molded differently, but we become less willing to change. We learn what we learn; we believe what we believe, and we do what we do, and that's good enough. It's been working for us, it's comfortable, and it's familiar. What if everything that we knew about ourselves and the world was wrong? Obviously, this is more of an objective viewpoint, as each of us is experiencing reality subjectively.

What if you were to trade places with someone around the world; perhaps someone within a remote tribe in Africa, or South America? This individual is now in your body, with your family, embodying the beliefs that were indoctrinated to you, and you are in their body, with their family, living out the beliefs and way of living passed down by their tribe's lineage. Who has the "right" way of living, and who has the "wrong" way of living? Now that you are in their shoes, wouldn't you consider your tribe's way of living normal, and the way to live life? Wouldn't you think that the individual that is now living in your family's home, enjoying modern technology, adopting the religion that your family has been practicing, and hanging out with your friends might have things mixed up?

We all think that our way of viewing things is the best way. Logically, we all can't have the best way of viewing things, right? If we have the best way, then that automatically makes someone else's perspective wrong, right? What if, and please indulge me for a moment, but what if we are ALL RIGHT and yet we are ALL WRONG?

This is part of the program. If we only look at our lives as being right or wrong, then we will stay in the program forever. We must open our mind to the idea of non-duality. We must open our minds to the idea that if a certain way of thinking, feeling, believing, and behaving works for one person or groups of people, then it can work for you as well. Also, having the understanding that because something has been working for you, doesn't mean it's the best way for you. It's important to know that ALL people have value for you if you are open to receiving it.

We only know what we know, and we don't know what we don't know. I want to emphasize that, "We only know what we know, and we don't know what we don't know." This means we must learn, grow, and evolve in our way of thinking, and in the way our core beliefs run our lives. Most people think that just because they have thought a certain way their whole lives; that means they have to keep thinking that way forever. That is false. This goes the same with our belief systems. Most of us have outdated belief systems that are no longer serving us.

Opening your mind is all about shedding off any beliefs or ideas that are no longer serving you, replacing them with ones that empower and uplift your way of being.

How did this concept help transform my life? I spent my life like most people and hung on to what I knew. I wasn't looking to change my mind about what I believed or how I lived. But when Michael died, I couldn't live the same life. I needed something different to happen. I was open emotionally and spiritually, which goes along with two of the other components of actualizing potential, connecting to your heart and awakening your soul; we will touch on those in a moment. I wasn't sure how to move forward in life. I was asking a bunch of questions I had never asked. I didn't have the answers. Seeking the answers put me on a path of exploration, learning, and discovery.

I don't know if you can relate to this, but as a kid in school, I hated to read. It always petrified me that the teacher would call on me during group reading. My self-talk was telling me I sucked at reading. I'm a slower reader, and I don't understand what I read. Maybe that was true, but only because I accepted it to be true. When the teacher would call on me, it seemed as if I blacked out. I didn't remember reading my paragraph. As I would read, I heard chuckles from my classmates following words I misread, or the murmurs over how slow I was reading. It was a scar that I carried with me. Even at home, my sisters and my mom would tease my dad about his reading ability, so I automatically adopted the belief that since my dad wasn't a good reader then obviously I'm not a good reader. I told myself over and over that, "Hey, I might not be book smart, but damn, I'm street smart."

I repeated this to myself throughout school. I mean, I was a jock, so I didn't need to spend my time reading. It was one or the other.

Despite my lack of reading ability, school came pretty easily to me. I earned mostly A's and B's. I had good test-taking skills, using the process of elimination and common sense. I never needed to study; I copied most of my work, and created a great rapport with my teachers—without needing to read a single book, well, maybe two books over 15 years. Not bad, huh?

I was actually a good learner. I associated not being a good reader, and not enjoying the process of school the same as not being a good learner. I didn't realize how intelligent I was until I learned I was more of an auditory learner. Some people have a photographic memory, but I had a tad bit of an audio graphic memory. I could remember almost anything that I heard and could recite it for a short period.

When I discovered this, I was in this phase of my life where my mind was open. I was asking questions and seeking answers. I would go on YouTube and start listening to inspirational videos, educational videos, and learning what I could about meditation, chakras, and different religions. One day I was painting the master bedroom of our home, and a podcast popped up. I didn't even know what a podcast was but what I heard had so much value and inspired me to continue to listen to more videos by this influencer.

Tom Bilyeu, and his show, Impact Theory, helped me fall in love with learning. Impact Theory is an interview series that explores the mindsets of the world's highest achievers to learn their secrets of success. I went on a binge, watching every interview he had done from Impact Theory and Inside Quest. Tom was the co-creator of Quest Nutrition, a multi-billion dollar company, before selling his shares to create Impact Theory. His life's goal is to pull people out of the matrix through storytelling. He intends to create the next Disney with a twist, developing an empowering mindset as the core narrative of his storytelling.

The guests on his show have absolutely changed my life. Not only was I learning at a rapid rate from the interviews and his powerful questions, but I took it to the next level by purchasing the books of the guests and dove deep into their content. I didn't realize that you didn't have to read books, but you could listen to them instead. This was a game-changer. I became completely obsessed with learning. I was learning everything I could about everything I could; philosophy, stoicism, different religions, neural science, biology, positive psychology, sacred geometry, trauma, leadership, the Law of Attraction, habit building, nature, biographies, conspiracy theories, and so much more. I couldn't get enough. My mind was open and hungry, so I fed it with all that I could.

We create our life with the information that we have in our mind and we use the information that is stored in order to solve the variety of challenges we face. When we bring in more information, we now have a larger library of opportunities to solve the problems in a broader way, which in return can give us the opportunity to create a new life with the new information. Think about how much information you had as a ten-year-old to solve the problems that you were facing in your life. What if you had the knowledge that you have now for that ten-year-old? The same goes for the version that you are today. You are using a certain amount of knowledge to solve the challenges you are facing. When we open our mind to more knowledge, not defining the knowledge as right or wrong, but only as information to solve challenges, then we can use this knowledge more effectively.

Knowledge is great, but what is vastly more important than knowledge is what you DO with that knowledge. Without integrating what you learn with your behavior, knowledge is worthless and only feeds the ego. Again, I will speak more about aligning your behavior in the coming pages.

2. Connecting to your heart

Asking myself how I was feeling was new for me.

When I was growing up, I was not encouraged to feel my emotions, especially as a boy. I was always told to suck it up. I don't blame my parents for viewing emotions in such a negative way, as I'm sure their parents did the same to them. When Michael died, it ripped me open. I felt the subtleties of each of my emotions. At first, I didn't know what was going on within me. I cried over everything. I couldn't even watch a Disney movie without breaking down. I felt every happy moment, loving moment, sad moment, and everything in between.

I had to figure out how to navigate my emotions. I started learning more about the heart center. By using meditation every day, and then journaling about my experience, I could get extremely clear on how I felt emotionally and what thoughts were leading to my emotions. I was gaining a sense of emotional intelligence. The more I was gaining awareness around my feelings and emotions, the more I could connect with others on a deeper level. I was, for the first time in my life, empathetic towards how others felt.

The more that you tap into your emotions the more sensitive you are towards them when they show up. The best leaders in the world have a great deal of emotional intelligence. When we cannot deal with our emotions healthily, then we experience stress, anxiety, fear, anger, and depression. We are storing these emotions and not allowing them to express themselves naturally. By letting go, surrendering, and forgiving people and experiences that have a heavy and powerful emotion connected to them, you will then be freer and lighter in the release of that emotional energy.

By looking within to see how my body felt, I didn't just realize my emotions, but I also realized my energy. My relationship with the word energy was different. I saw how everything connects. Awareness of energy changed the way I approached everything I did in my life.

Nicola Tesla said, "If you want to find the secrets of the universe, think in terms of energy, frequency, and vibration." Everything around us is energy, frequency, and vibration. We are even energy, frequency, and vibration. When we experience energy, depending on the frequency of where the energy is vibrating at, it will determine the quality of the effects that the energy will have. We can understand the quality of the energy from our head down to our body. We must FEEL the subtleties of the electrical current flowing from the energy.

I realized how the energy of thoughts directly correlated with the energy of how my body felt; which had direct effects on my emotions, which led to my body performing a certain way with the type of actions I took daily. Everything was correlated. I took my awareness further by paying attention to how other people were affecting my energy. I learned how working out, learning, nature, laughing, meditation, and journaling were directly creating positive charges within my body. My energy rose, and I was aware of what made me feel expansive and what made me feel contractive, by how my body felt. This is the translation of energy. We can experience more of what life offers when we practice going beyond our five senses into the invisible realm to translate our environment. This was only possible because I opened my heart up to feeling and being more sensitive to the energy I allowed in and out of my heart center.

3. Awakening your soul

We are not here to work 40 hours a week for a corporation that doesn't give two shits about you or your family. They will replace you in a heartbeat, fire you if that is better for their bottom line, overwork you and underpay you. We are being used, abused, and are in modern day slavery, shackled by money. We need money to eat, to have a roof over our heads, to give birth, and even to die. I didn't even question why I was working as a food server until Michael died. I thought the point of working is to make money, and since I made six figures a year, I believed I was set. Well, that was no longer the case. Michael had passed. I no longer wanted to step into the same restaurant where we had once worked.

My soul was now awake, and I didn't want to work for the sake of money. I wanted to do something that gave me purpose. I wanted to live my life for meaning. I wanted to get paid for what I loved doing. Every. Single. Day.

To awaken your soul is to awaken the fire that has been dwelling within. It awakens you to purpose, to desire, to passion. We can have, do, and be whatever we want. We are limitless, but mustn't be afraid to ask for what we want. We were never told to dream big, but to play it safe and find a secure job. Anyone who lived through 2020 knows that there is no such thing as a secure job when you work for someone else. To maximise your potential, you must open up to your soul, the bigger part of you. This is The Inner Hero and you will learn much more about this part of yourself throughout this book, but you MUST tap into this part of yourself to actualize your potential. This is the part of yourself that pulls you forward when you are tired. This is the part of yourself that is excited to wake up every morning. Without a deep and passionate desire, you cannot actualize your potential. Why would you? You don't have the fuel to keep your engine running. Your soul is the fuel to your vessel, and without connecting deeply with your soul's purpose you will inevitably run on empty.

Something else happens when you awaken your soul. You learn the universe is a lot bigger than you once thought. It's much more intelligent and intricate than you once thought. There is an intelligence working behind the scenes to make sure each of our fingernails are growing, our hair is growing, the flowers are blooming; the clouds are forming; the tides are rising and falling; while the planets are circling the sun, the sun staying at the right temperature for us to not burn up or freeze, and so many other things that make my brain hurt when thinking about how intelligent this universe has to be for it to function the way it does. When we are awake to our soul, then we understand that same intelligent being that has built the universe and lives within and around everything in it, also built us, and lives within and around us. We are bigger than we have ever given ourselves credit for. We are magical, intelligent machines choosing what we want to create and pursue in our lives. We have to open our mind to new possibilities; realize the energy around us and how it makes us feel, and awaken to our soul's purpose. Awakening your soul is going from an unconscious being to a conscious being who is aware of the infinite love and intelligence of our soul's nature.

4. Aligning your behavior

Awareness is everything to me. If you are not aware, then you cannot intentionally make improvements in your life. Awareness is not enough though. Just the same, that knowledge is not power, but potential power. Awareness is the ability to see what needs to be done, but seeing is not enough. We must take action in our awareness. When we decide to align our behavior with what we want, then sustainable change presents itself to us.

Aligning your behavior is about creating an empowering routine in order to become the person you wish to be and to live the lifestyle you hope to live. Repetition is how we change our brain, body, and belief systems. "We are what we repeatedly do. Excellence is, then, not an act, but a habit." - Aristotle.

We must build habits around what we learn and build actionable steps around the awareness that we gain. Another way to say this is to embody or integrate what we are learning. It's different to conceptualize and understand something compared to embodying that same knowledge. There's a difference in being aware of the bad-habit that needs to change, and taking consistent daily steps in changing the bad-habit into a good-habit.

We must remember that there is work to be done, and aligning our behavior to what we want is us doing the work. Being consistent in this process will absolutely help you actualize your potential, as it has helped me in the past and consistently helps me to move forward. The more that I have been able to align my behaviors, the more I lead by example because I am embodying my values, living within my integrity, pursuing my passions, and by being the man I intentionally created.

CHAPTER 8
THE SHEDDING

I was seeing dramatic changes throughout the first year of my transformation. In the first half I felt awful, depressed, lost, and alone. I knew I couldn't stay that way, so I continued to turn to those newly discovered tools, to love myself more and actualize my potential to live a fuller life.

The tools didn't work overnight, but I held on to my faith. I stayed persistent in my journey, taking courageous action toward purpose, happiness, and health. There is a process at work behind the scenes, and it was important for me to continue the work—because the work, works.

I saw a difference in how I was showing up and how I was treating other people. I was more compassionate and accepting. Combining these tools had this medicinal and healing effect. I was open to changing every aspect of my life—from the core of who I believed I was, to someone making a difference.

One challenging aspect of this transformation was my attachment to Christianity. I had spent my life practicing this religion. I wasn't someone who said they were Christian just to have a religion while not practicing the beliefs. Being a Christian for me wasn't a safety net.

I was a devoted Christian. I went to church every week, prayed every day, and was part of small groups. A small group is a fellowship among individuals from the church that discuss the Bible or specific topics that help improve life. It's an intimate deep-dive, creating closer relationships amongst church members. It's like a mastermind for the church. There are different small groups. I was in a men's group and together with my wife in a couple's group.

When I was younger, I felt that one day I was going to be a pastor. I was a pretty good Christian, but not perfect by any means. I felt pride in not judging people because I didn't want to be judged.

When I would have conversations with different people, as soon as I mentioned I was a Christian, they would completely shift. I felt they acted differently toward me, closing themselves off, or apologizing for cussing, while I was also cussing.

I didn't cuss to fit in. I don't think cuss words are necessarily bad words. Maybe it's in the context, but I believe there are worse words than shit or hell. Here are a few bad words or phrases that I don't allow in my home or in my mind. "I hate you." "I'm stupid." "I can't do it." "You suck." These words and phrases are more acceptable in society, yet far more harmful than typical cuss words. I won't diminish myself or others—this is a crime against loving our humanity.

People would shift behaviour as soon as I mentioned I was a Christian. If I were with other Christians, they would become more self-righteous and act like they were better than others. They would put us on a pedestal.

If they were not Christian, they treated me as an innocent child in the world. No longer were they being themselves, but trying to be someone else. They suddenly put on a mask. There is a stereotype or identity around having a Christian title, and people try to accommodate it by wearing that false mask. I could feel that some people felt insecure, while others would judge me for my faith. Either way, this was why I intentionally tried to not judge others for their beliefs. I didn't want to be judged for my beliefs.

In reality, I was being judged on the title of my religion. Depending on their perspective on Christianity, determined how they viewed me. Perhaps they saw me as a caring and loving person like Christ or self-righteous and judging, as many Christians behave. People are unique, as are all Christians, but people don't understand that.

•

Michael's death ripped me open spiritually. I put everything I had ever known or learned about Christianity into question. Who was God? What was God? How does God work? Who was Jesus? Why was He so important? What was the point of the cross? These were a few of my questions regarding my faith.

If you asked me these questions a year before Michael died, I would give you specific and detailed answers with the utmost confidence. I KNEW the answers without a doubt. I was in a different place now, and rather than wanting to spew out answers the church or someone else gave me, I wanted to know the answers to these questions by looking within, and other areas outside of the Bible, to discover how my inner discernment felt about my questions.

Prior to my transformation, these existential questions were subject to my confirmation bias. Confirmation bias means that you will interpret evidence in a way where it adds to your belief about a subject, while ignoring the evidence if it goes against your belief. Most of us have confirmation biases about spiritual and political beliefs. We don't view belief systems through a neutral lens when we allow confirmation bias to take control. We build up evidence to strengthen what we already believe, while dismissing evidence that would go against what we believe. It's kind of fucked up if you think about it. I spent my life using confirmation bias when asking existential questions—I received answers to validate what I wanted to believe.

This time was different. I wanted to know the truth. If we pride ourselves on being right rather than discovering the truth, we will fight to not be wrong. Maybe, just maybe I had been wrong about everything? If I wasn't wrong, then it would strengthen my beliefs. If wrong, then I could shift directions toward a path that served my higher self. I knew it was time to become uncomfortable with my spirituality. It was time to give permission to question my faith.

I didn't begin this process as, "I need to question my beliefs." It was more like, "Things aren't adding up. My beliefs don't feel like they completely make sense to me anymore." I didn't choose my beliefs. I adopted them from someone else.

With my faith rattled, I would constantly pray for healing, guidance, direction, truth, awareness, openness, love, strength, and answers to understand what I was feeling and experiencing. Following my prayers, I would meditate, and in quieting my mind, I could hear that tiny whisper behind my thoughts. I would journal about my faith, the questions, and my theories of what I thought were the answers.

Not only did I continue to study the Bible, but I also dove into different religious texts and philosophies such as Hinduism, Buddhism, Taoism, Stoicism, Atheism, and other isms. I plunged into Abraham-Hicks regarding the Law of Attraction, different sciences, energy work, metaphysics, mythology, and various healing modalities such as Theta Healing and the Orion Effect. I completely embraced personal development and self-help.

I didn't get sucked into any one belief system because I didn't sit in any category. I could go in and out of each one without attachment. I saw the commonality between each belief system, even between belief systems that seem to contradict, such as Christianity and atheism.

We aren't that different, after all.

Every religion and philosophy is an expression of one's understanding of life. There is not just one way of understanding, as consciousness is here to expand and understand itself through us. As there are various foods, plants, animals, colors, and terrains, various human beings have various thoughts and beliefs. That means God, consciousness, source energy, The Great Spirit, or the universe has a way to connect to the diversity of its creation. God evolves with us as the universe continues expanding, yet this energy of creation has been the same since the beginning of time and will be the same everlasting. As humans evolve and need different understandings about God, we are given different perspectives or units of measurement to explain All That Is.

I learned that whatever created our existence is still alive, still present, and still consciously expanding. This energy force is active in our lives and acts in the world today more than we can understand. This energy binds all the physical and the non-physical at the atomic level and the universal level. The evidence of this creator shows up in patterns, fractals, seasons, and cycles. God is not an old white man with a beard. God is the Source of all Creation, as energy, the energy that is omnipresent, meaning it is within everything, everywhere, at the same time.

We find this energy in all that exists. Perhaps we must reframe how we understand and see what we might call God as something much grander, much more intricate, much more intelligent than how we have defined it previously. This is a life force that is eternal and consistent. When we connect and align with this life force, we feel whole, purposeful, and complete. When we disconnect from this source energy, we feel lost, confused, and uncertain.

I had always found it interesting that before the modern age, before we were all connected through instant information, before we had access to other parts of the world, before we could travel by plane, or before we traveled to the corners of the world by ship, that specific belief systems were in every tribe, village, and community.

We can go back to the Egyptians, Mayans, Native Americans, Greeks, tribes in the Himalayas, and to any ancient part of the world, and understand that they each held different but specific rituals, practices, and beliefs around some unseen force of energy. This energy was present in their culture. They worshiped it, prayed to it, sacrificed to it, gave thanks to it, and named it. They all created rules and laws around how to have a relationship with it, and respect and honor it. Perhaps they have different names, but the feeling, and the energy of this life force was the same.

The only difference was how each culture interpreted this life force. In my self-discovery, I had to ask whether these cultures were wrong or right? Maybe it has little to do with right and wrong? Perhaps it is an intelligent energy force, an intimate relationship with all parts of itself, consciously connected to all of its Creation?

Whether it's within the plant world, animal world, human world, cellular networks, or planetary networks, this energy is consciously at work, and WE get to decide what that means for us. The name is irrelevant, but the alignment and connection with IT is everything. When we can deeply connect, we understand WE are IT. We extend the source of creation that has met us at this leading edge of expansion. God is continuing to create through us. We are the vessel of this life force. Consciousness remembers this truth on a grand scale in this time and space.

I hope to inspire you to explore your faith or lack of faith to understand what you believe, and why you believe or don't believe. This is not about making anyone believe in anything specific, but about creating self-awareness of one's belief system. I support you in whatever you choose, and hope to empower you to strengthen that relationship. I hope it uplifts you, inspires you, and guides you toward truth, love, and expansion.

•

When I was exploring my spirituality, I focused more on Jesus than on other religions or people who I was studying. I wanted to understand Him, and His influence on our society. I couldn't grasp or understand the significance of the cross, other than its metaphorical side. Through a Christian lens I understood, but I was trying to view it objectively. What I discovered was the representation of the death of self, the time in between, and the awakening. This is what it looks like in the process of enlightenment. This is also the process of nature in seasons. Summer is life, fall is death, winter is in-between, and spring is the rebirth. Either way, I decided that the understanding of the death and resurrection of Christ might never make sense to me, or I might never in my lifetime receive the answer. I would put that part on hold. I was okay with the fact that perhaps His story of how it was told in the Bible is true, or maybe it wasn't, but it didn't have to define the way I wanted to live.

Instead, I focused on how Jesus lived his life, how He accepted people, loved the unlovable, forgave the wrongdoers, and connected to the divine energy called God in that period. Jesus perhaps, was the ultimate vessel and came to teach us how to allow the energy that created All That Is to flow through us. Buddha was another teacher, all loving and healing. I don't know the answer, and maybe I'll never know, but I know that it's okay. I don't believe that we will be punished if we don't have all the answers—we aren't supposed to have all answers. Find the answers that feel good for you and help you live a more full and empowered life. If your belief system disempowers you or holds you captive, then it's time to break out of that box. Your spirituality is intimate and specific. It is as intimate and personalized to each of us, just as our thumbprint is uniquely designed.

I felt overwhelmingly excited about this newfound understanding of my belief system, but I knew that not everyone would share in the same excitement. The more I learned, the more I wanted to share with others, including my wife and mother. It was important to share with my wife because we married under Christian Law. The oath we had taken was in alignment with a specific belief system.

My new belief system didn't go against our marriage, but it was a step in the wrong direction in her eyes. I remember the day I told her. She looked at me through eyes of sadness. I felt like I let her down and betrayed her. I was trying to find my truth, but it compromised her truth and the truth we had with each other. This was the start of when we disconnected and moved in different directions.

My wife wasn't the only one I felt obligated to tell. I had to let my spiritual best friend, my mom, know what I was thinking and feeling. I had a tougher time speaking with my mother about this than I did with my wife. I saw how it affected my wife's relationship with me, and I didn't want this to create a wedge in the relationship I had with my mom.

So, I wrote a letter to her. Perhaps a letter would translate more clearly my experiences than I had verbally communicated to my wife. I read the letter to my mom in person, giving her some time to speak her truth.

What I received was what I expected, but not what I hoped for. My mother shared a similar perspective with my wife. They felt betrayed. They saw me as someone lost, wandering through the desert. My mother told me she was afraid for my soul and wouldn't support me on my path. This broke my heart. I looked back at the experience we had at Baja Fresh, connecting and expanding on our ideas of who and what God is, and now we no longer saw eye to eye.

Reflecting on how dramatically different my past religious beliefs were to my new beliefs, I could understand why my mother and wife reacted the way they did. I went from a devoted Christian to no religion. I was open to all beliefs, yet attached to none. No wonder they thought I was lost. But what I knew from the year of deep diving into faith was that I was clearer than I had ever been. I was awake and moving toward my purpose. I had to accept this and be okay with no one understanding.

It's scary to speak the truth to those closest to you, especially if it goes against their beliefs. It shook my relationship with my mother for a few years. I wasn't sure if we would get back to where we connected before. I had to compromise in order to speak my truth. I can't control how people respond when I live out and speak what I believe to be true.

If we worry about what others think, fear of being judged will imprison our lives. I believe my relationship with my mother now is the best it's ever been because we had the hard conversations.

The closest people to us can sometimes hold us captive. We want them to love and accept us, hoping to receive their approval. We bend over backwards, denying our own truth to avoid being abandoned or exiled. If it were strangers, then we wouldn't care. We would say fuck it and speak our truth. With family though, we try to conform as much as we can.

We must be willing to lose everything we love; the attachment to the conditions of love that go against our true nature. Love of the ones closest to us. Love of religion. Love of our identity. This includes materialistic love. We must lose everything that we attach love to, so we can be free to allow ourselves to uncover the love within.

Will we ever be 100% authentically ourselves? Probably not, but we must practice as much as possible, and paradoxically, the most challenging time to practice is with those closest to us.

If you speak your truth unapologetically, lovingly, then you will be free, and those who love you will accept you. If not, perhaps it's not about you. Maybe it's about their trials and tribulations within their beliefs? When we speak our truth, it shakes up their belief systems and challenges their way of thinking. Let them feel challenged. Your truth is for you, and their truth, for them.

What is your truth? Are you brave enough to speak it out loud? What will it take for you to be authentically YOU? I believe it's time to take off another mask. Do you? Speaking your truth has little to do with spirituality, but honoring, valuing, and loving yourself enough to speak from the depths of your heart.

Shedding the mask that's holding you back from being the hero will inevitably give you the confidence to put on your cape in every situation life throws your way. Look inside, be courageous enough to ask the hard questions, and be honest about the answers. The one in the mirror deserves your complete authenticity.

I'm encouraging you to understand that there are no black and white answers, but there are possible answers. Asking the hard questions can help you find what the answers might be. It's exploration and discovery. It's about brainstorming or creating theories about the answers to your questions.

CHAPTER 9

DISCOVERING PURPOSE

How do you discover your purpose? I believe purpose comes in different ways.

One way is that the universe sprinkles little breadcrumbs throughout your life, and those breadcrumbs are signs telling you what you might be passionate about, and what you are passionate about is what usually aligns you to your purpose.

Sometimes it's hard to see, and only in hindsight can you connect the pieces of the puzzle, making sense of the bigger picture. Some people are born with a specific passion, while others are told by their parents or teachers what direction to move toward. Then there are some whose passion is born from anger. They see a wrong in the world and fight to make it right. But for most of us, the way we find passion is to explore what we love and enjoy doing, while also highlighting the set of skills we are good at.

If your breadcrumbs aren't clear, and the road signs don't match up, it's okay. It's time to take action by choosing a direction and to stick with it long enough to understand whether it is right for you. Adjust and adapt with every step along the way. Where we start and where we intend to end up might be, and most likely will be, in different locations, because the more we dive into our specific passions, the more we learn about what we like and dislike.

If you said that you wanted to be a teacher, then what do you want to teach? There are an infinite amount of subjects to teach, many levels and grades to teach, and many locations to teach. The more you dive into what you believe is your passion, the closer you get. There isn't a purpose assigned to you—you get to create a purpose. Some passions are clear and direct for certain people, and sometimes passions are buried under a pile of mud. You can wait around for it to show itself, but you might wait a lifetime.

I encourage you to explore the self and discover what lights you up, so the lotus flower can be seen. Your passion and purpose is the lotus flower. It's there, just underneath the surface of the mud.

•

There was a specific day when I sat down to meditate. I created an intention of asking a certain question. My intention was to know what I wanted to do with my life. The question I asked was, "If money was not a factor, but I still had to work at something, what would I love and enjoy doing for the rest of my life?"

To go with this question, I erased the aspect of time. If I get hooked up on what today looks like, then I might miss out on the possibilities of tomorrow.

I was lacking resources and skill sets. By taking time out of the equation and looking forward to my future ideal-self, I could gain the resources and skill sets I needed. If it took me 20 years to become masterful at whatever I dedicated my life to, then I would embody it for the rest of my life.

I create certain intentions before I meditate, whether it's asking a specific question or maybe I want to feel calm after a stressful day. Either way, it's a good idea to get in the habit of intention setting. I go as far as creating intentions before almost everything I do in my day.

I began doing this after learning of a powerful concept known as Segment Intending, created by author and teacher Abraham-Hicks. Segment Intending is where you make intentions prior to starting a segment in your day. You create an intention before you get in the car, before you go to the grocery store, before you have lunch with a friend, before an interview, before going to bed, or before anything.

I chose one of my favorite YouTube meditations using binaural beats. If you are unfamiliar with binaural beats, then I recommend checking it out. I use them for meditations, studying, writing, and reading. You must wear headphones for it to work. In your right ear, you will hear a constant vibratory sound that is set at a specific frequency that may sound like, waaaaaaaa. In your left ear, it is set at a different frequency that might sound like wuuuuuuu. When you put the earbuds in, you will get a sound like wauwauwauwauwau, which changes the frequency of your brain waves. You can go from beta to alpha to theta in a matter of minutes. So, when pairing this technology with meditation, you can get deep, really fast.

In the beginning of my meditations, I like to allow my "monkey brain" to have space to do what it does, vent, complain, think about problems, what I did moments before my meditation, and what I am planning after my meditation.

I continue to breathe slowly in and out, allowing my thoughts to race, and in between each thought, I bring my attention back to my breath. With each breath, my thoughts are slower. My mind is no longer racing. It is becoming calm, present, and grounded. My awareness heightens. I stop focusing so much on the clutter that exists on the surface and direct my focus inward. I check in with myself regarding how I am feeling, whether there's any heaviness or tightness within my body. If I am experiencing this, then I ask myself what emotions am I experiencing in those areas, and feel inside of that space by acknowledging those emotions for being there, validating those emotions for why they showed up, thanking those emotions for communicating with me, then letting go of those emotions as they are no longer needed.

The heaviness feels lighter, and the tightness softens. I repeat this process as many times as necessary, from the top of my head down to my toes. When finished with my toes, I send my awareness into the earth to feel grounded, back up to my heart, expand my awareness into the room, the surrounding walls, then as far out and up as I can. I visualize my home in its entirety, then my neighborhood, my city, my country, the earth, and as far up and out as I can consciously visualize, passing by planets, galaxies, suns, and dimensions. Sometimes I end up in a place that is embodied with complete emptiness; it's pitch black. The silence is deafening; the stillness is freeing; I blend into the nothingness, and in that space I am ONE with everything that exists. Sometimes, instead of it being pitch black, it's a blinding white light.

Other times I am overlooking the ocean from a cliff. Golden clouds cover the ocean; the sun is rising or setting; I know it doesn't matter because I know that the sun doesn't rise; it is perceived to rise, and the sun doesn't set; it is perceived to set in this space, but they are both eternal, with no beginning and no end. Behind me is a whimsical forest, full of magic, and full of love. Roots of the trees go in and out of the forest floor, connecting all the trees as if they were holding hands. There are rivers and streams that offer everlasting life, which wash away all that burdens me. When I put my head into the water, I can show up somewhere else, as in, there is another world underneath the water. Moss grows everywhere with a fluorescent vibrant green shade. There are lagoons that offer waterfalls falling from the heavens. Different animals come to visit me. Sometimes it's a white deer with the biggest antlers that I have ever seen, while other times it's a purple lion with gigantic wings.

Perhaps my mind is making all of this up? I have a vivid imagination. Maybe I am being visited by God, angels, or my spirit animals? Who knows, I could be entering my personal heaven where I get to interact with All That Is. Either way, when I am in these states of consciousness, I feel safe; I receive love and healing, and the whisper behind my monkey mind becomes louder while answering my questions.

If you can visualize something in your mind, and feel something in your body creating an emotional response, then who's to say it's not reality? A dream is a reality—not of this reality, where it is experienced within our five senses, but it's a reality beyond our senses, perhaps of a different dimension?

I try not to define it so much, but observe and experience the beauty of this higher-conscious realm, or the unique imagination that is being expressed by my mind. They are both equally magical and awe-inspiring.

When I reach this state of consciousness, I will return to the question that I asked before I started the meditation. On this day, again, I asked, "If money was not a factor, but I still had to work at something, what would I love and enjoy doing for the rest of my life?"

A dialogue formulated in my head. When this first happened, it felt like I was making it up, but the more I allowed it to flow, the more I realized this was not me creating this dialogue, but it was me interacting with another part of myself, a deeper part of myself, a more expansive part of myself.

It's possible that my conscious mind is communicating with my subconscious mind, or it could be my higher self, angels, guides, ancestors, or more. How it's labeled or defined isn't as important as the emotional and relational experience that manifests in the desired results, within the alignment of your values and moral compass.

What I mean is that if I use the word God to define my experience, it can be understood differently by other humans. For example, we have used the name of God for not only love and healing, but also war and genocide.

What is more important to understand? The wolf in sheep's clothing, and calling it a sheep, or seeing, hearing, and feeling the truth behind the illusion? The name does not matter as much as the universal truth that unconditionally aligns us with nature.

The dialogue began slowly, and then built momentum. Here's what that conversation sounded like:

Me: If money was not a factor, but I still had to work at something, what would I love and enjoy doing for the rest of my life?

IS (Inner Self): What have I always loved and enjoyed doing that I was good at?

Me: I'm good with people and I love connecting with them, real estate, maybe? Both my sisters are in that industry, plus my dad has remodeled and flipped homes. I recently redid my home, but it was not the most fun. If I get good enough at it though, I can make enough money so that I could spend my time traveling. I love traveling.

IS: So if that was the case, I would sell houses, buy houses, or renovate them, not because I love and enjoy it, but for the money that comes along with this career. With the money, then I would get to travel around the world doing and enjoying what I loved. That defeats the purpose of this exercise because I already make six figures a year and travel a lot. Take money out of the equation and focus on what I love and enjoy doing. Whether I fail or succeed at it doesn't matter because I want to get better and better at whatever "it" is.

Me: I love playing sports, and I was good. I loved the competitive nature of them and I loved how much I would always improve. I was also the leader of all the teams that I have ever played on. I'm 25 so

I'll cross professional athlete off the list. Maybe there's something else with sports, though?

IS: What about a coach?

Me: Yeah, I could coach. But I have helped coach before, and I didn't have fun doing it. I love sports, but it's about the participation of the sport that makes me feel alive, not observing sports. I would rather play than coach.

IS: I'm an outstanding leader, and people enjoy following me. I am already in the food and beverage industry, maybe taking on a leadership role?

Me: I have lost all passion for the hospitality industry. I would be good at that job but I would work more hours, while missing holidays, and have less freedom to travel. Also, I foresee myself more or less babysitting rather than leading. So I definitely don't want to do that.

IS: I wanted to be a pastor when I was younger. What drew me to thinking about being a pastor?

Me: I want to help people. I also know that my relationship with God has helped me stay focused on my path and to stay morally grounded. I never felt like my calling was in the church though, because those who are in the church have found their guidance. I have always been attracted to the ones who were lost, or curious for more. Especially now that I don't feel connected to any specific religion, but what would I pastor?

IS: I went to school for a semester for elementary education. I have always been drawn to helping kids. Maybe I should go back to school?

Me: I didn't like that semester of school. I think I would take my work home with me. It would be hard to see the kids that I want to help but I wouldn't be able to intervene. I know that I would have somewhat of an influence on them, but I don't feel passionate about teaching the subjects that are being taught in school. I would rather teach kids about the lessons of life. Plus, I don't want to travel only in the summer. I want freedom to travel whenever I want.

IS: So far, I would like to have the freedom to travel, teach lessons about life, help people, be a leader of some sort, and be a participant in whatever I'm doing, rather than the observer. I feel like I'm getting closer. What is one of my favorite things to talk about when I am drinking or smoking weed with my friends? What conversations light me up?

Me: I love talking about life, and how to improve our lives. I enjoy the expansiveness of these conversations with friends and family. It seems like when I'm taking part in these conversations, me and whoever I'm speaking with are connecting on a much deeper level. People always feel comfortable talking about their problems and challenges with me. They look forward to hearing my perspective on the matter and hope that I can give them advice. Now that I think about it, people have always sought me out for advice since I was young. I liked to be in that position. I think that's what makes me an outstanding leader; that I am living out the advice that I give to others. I have always led by example and I don't judge others for where they are at. I am happy with the life that I have created and I can help others to create their life. I think I'm pretty good at life. I bought a home at a young age. I make substantial money. I got married at a young age. I've traveled to 19 different countries. I have made good investments financially, and I believe I'm a genuinely kind-hearted person. I am good at life.

IS: That would be cool if I could coach life.

Me: Yeah, coach life. That would be cool, but that's a made up job. I can't do that.

IS: What else could I do?

Me: I have found that writing is enjoyable to me. I am writing every day and it has only made me more aware and connected to myself.

IS: If I could make up a job that doesn't exist, what would it be?

Me: Oh, I love that question. Wait! I would like to coach life. Yeah, coach life. That feels good when I say that. Hang on, coach life? I think it's something that already exists. I think they call that a life coach? Hmm, I'm going to have to look that up after I finish this meditation. I like the sound of that though, and I feel excited to see what I find out about life coaching.

IS: We are complete.

From there, the dialogue ended. No more questions came up, and no more answers. The only thing I felt in that moment was this magnetic force pulling me towards researching what the fuck a life coach is? I did not know if life coaching was real or not, but I had heard that term somewhere.

I spent a few more moments finishing my meditation in silence and gave gratitude for the conversation with my inner self.

After 20 minutes of meditation, I ran straight to the computer and looked up the term life coach. I clicked the first link that popped up, "iPEC," (Institute for Professional Excellence in Coaching). This is a world-renowned coaching program. I went through all the resources they offered to learn about life coaching, the program's values, ideologies, and methodologies, and what coaching is not. I read studies about the benefits of coaching for businesses, family, relationships, and for overall life satisfaction.

Everything I was reading felt like I was reading about myself.

My heart was racing and grabbing on to every word. I kept thinking to myself, "Wow, this is me. They are describing me. This is what I want to do for the rest of my life."

I couldn't understand how this had never crossed my path, but for the first time in my life I found something outside of sports to connect to that was worth dedicating my time and energy in a noble pursuit.

Life coaching is something I could grow and develop—it's something that would allow me to work remotely, which means I get to pick my schedule. I can be home for the holidays. I can travel. I can make a difference in other people's lives, and I can be a leader enhancing my life through the tools and teachings of this life coaching program. It seemed pretty perfect. I decided at that moment I was going to set up an appointment with the administration's coach, and if it went well, talk to my wife about registering with this training institute.

•

I love how life unfolds, and how the universe brings together moments of synchronicities, or how God shows you when you are on the right path. Writing about this experience brings so much emotion up for me, as this was such a monumental opportunity for me.

Within the first moments of my call with the administration coach at iPEC, I knew I was going to be part of this program. I had a handful of questions for the young man on the phone. He was a few years younger than me. I wanted to hear how he decided on life coaching, and what he believed was his bigger purpose. He always felt like he wanted to make a difference. He was a high achiever and things came easily to him. He naturally understood how things worked, how energy worked, and how success worked. At one time he wanted to be a lawyer, or a doctor to make a lot of money, but he read a book that changed his life when he was in high school, *How To Win Friends, And Influence People* by Dale Carnegie. After reading that book, he understood he was here to empower others to live a more satisfied and fulfilled life. Goosebumps popped all over my body—that was the exact moment when I received confirmation that I was going to be a life coach.

How To Win Friends, And Influence People, was the book I was reading. Out of all the books in existence, that was the book the young man said changed his life, and inspired him to be a life coach—the book I was reading! There is no such thing as coincidences, but ALIGNMENT. I was on the right path, and nothing was going to stop me now.

Exploration is a big part of discovering your passion. Sometimes you don't know what you like until you do it more than once. Sometimes it takes a hundred times until you learn you don't like something. I wanted different results, so I was doing as many activities and routines as I could. If you want your life to change, then you must change what you do daily.

It was no surprise then, after telling my wife that I wanted to join this program, she felt hesitant. She reminded me that every week I was doing something different. One week I'm learning about stocks, the next I'm doing meditation, after that I'm doing yoga, diving into different religions, looking into different network marketing programs, learning about wine and beer to advance in hospitality, and so on. She thought I might be a little lost and confused. I understood where she was coming from, but this was one thing that I felt completely certain—I was meant for this. We came to an agreement. Since life coaching was something that I wanted to do for the rest of my life, waiting one year would be nothing in the scheme of time. I agreed I would learn as much as I could during the year about life coaching, and if I still felt certain at the end, then I would sign up and pay $10k for this program.

I read as many books as I could that year. I studied spirituality, energy work, life coaching, and did a basic certification through a $2.00 online course. I didn't care about the price of the course. I was hungry and driven to learn at an aggressive rate. I listened to over 1000 hours of podcasts in that year. I have never learned or grown so much intellectually in such a short period. My brain was like a sponge and it couldn't download enough information.

With all this information, I would journal every day to express what I was learning to digest what I was feeding my mind. These writings eventually turned into blogs, writing inspirational content on social media throughout that year, and calling it *The Daily Dugan*. Corny I know, but I loved it, and it was filling up my cup. People I worked with started calling me The Daily Dugan. Some of them were definitely talking shit through sarcasm, which I acted oblivious to, giving them a big smile and a chuckle.

Others though, on countless occasions, would pull me aside and express intimate gratitude towards my messages. Sometimes people would tear up when they told me they needed to hear what I had written, and how it pulled them out of a negative loop. I realized people were hungry for this positive light I had found, and now I was someone who could be the bridge to these individuals.

CHAPTER 10
TAKING COURAGEOUS ACTION

After a week's long solo trip to Yosemite National Park, 15 months after deciding I wanted to become a life coach, I sat down with my wife and expressed that it was time for me to move forward to the next part of coaching.

I needed to develop deeper and expansive skill sets, while also learning more about the business aspect of coaching. Timing is a funny thing, because two days later we found out that we were pregnant. We were having our first baby, after trying for more than a year. If I didn't speak up days before, I believe I wouldn't have after finding out that news. I was getting ready to spend a lot of money on this program, and wasn't sure if it was appropriate to spend that type of money before having a baby.

Decisions are powerful. As my father always told me, "Life is full of decisions." It was a simple phrase he said again and again while I would respond with, "Yep, I know," and slightly roll my eyes.

Now that I'm older, I understand what he meant. Each decision adds up, creates momentum, and forms your reality. There are thousands of decisions we make every day, some unconsciously through our autopilot, and some consciously. To live consciously is to be aware of as many of these micro moments in which you have to decide something. Viktor Frankl, in his book, *Man's Search For Meaning* writes, "Between stimulus and response there is a space. In that space is our power to choose our response. In our response lie our growth and our freedom."

So, what does it mean to decide? What is it to have decisiveness when deciding within the power of choice? It is to have awareness and consideration in the space of stimulus and response. Your response brings a resolution or conclusion to a subject or experience.

When you decide to move in a specific direction, that is the conclusion. That is the direction you chose, the direction you take action toward. It is indecision that kills action and momentum. When we decide, it is important to understand the power at hand and how to make the macro decisions, aka the BIG decisions. The question I had to propose after finding out we were having a baby is whether I should stick with this program or wait until it is more convenient. The better question to ask myself is whether the decision that I was about to make was a conscious-based decision or a fear-based decision.

There are two things I have known about myself since I was a young boy. First, I wanted to make a difference in the world, and second, I wanted to be a father.

Now, both were coming true at the same time. This realization of being a father definitely lit a fire under me. If I waited on life coaching, was I waiting out of fear of not having enough money, or consciously deciding to wait because I felt that it truly wasn't the right time? The decision that I had to make came easily to me. It was time to double down. It was time to get focused and put my all into this coaching program, because I knew that if I took courageous action, then I could have both if I wholeheartedly invested my energy.

All the studying that I invested in the year prior to this program paid off. I was prepared and ready to be a coach. I studied even more in the next year during this program. I not only had to study these new principles, tools, and concepts, but they had to be practiced in real time.

Through the program, I worked with three personal life coaches, and I was also coaching someone. I would go to Los Angeles every three months to do three, 12 hour a day intensive workshops. This was deep and healing work.

I had discovered my people. Not that I didn't have amazing friends and family I loved and cared for, and that they had been part of my life since I could remember, but there's something about having the power to choose a group of like-minded people with ambitious goals, who have the determination to achieve those goals through their actions.

Tribe is one pillar where lasting change happens, where sustained change happens. We have all heard that we are the average of the five people that we spend the most time with. The more you can be around people with similar ambitions, beliefs, and passions, people who inspire and empower you, the more you can morph or upgrade your productivity and results. The more that we spend our time around people who are lazy, unmotivated, discouraged and gossip about others, have disempowering beliefs, perverted thoughts, limited perspective, amongst many other traits that you might imagine, then we too, will start becoming that type of person. Maybe not today, or even tomorrow, but eventually you will start becoming the average of that group.

I believe we do this because we are adaptable creatures. We adapt to our environments. We have a field of energy, like an invisible bubble around us. As we spend time and space with friends or family, our bubbles can merge and become entangled with one another. When our field is influenced, we are influenced, whether it is in a negative or positive way. Let me be clear, when I mention negative and positive, I'm not referring to good or bad. Those are judgements based on an individual's belief systems. There is no good or bad, but our thoughts and beliefs make something good or bad. When I speak of negative or positive, I refer to the energetic charge of something. Negative charges can lower your energy and break down your mind and body, creating sickness, and cause a lack of emotional excitement for life. Positive charges allow the body and mind to heal, promoting eagerness and excitement for life, and may have a lightness about life as if the sun is always shining.

Keep this in mind; these are the higher ends of the positive charge and the lower ends of the negative charge. These vibrational charges are constantly dancing with one another in between these extremes. We elevate or lower our base resonating level by many influences. The frequency of our resonating vibration shifts, depending on the strength of influence within the other vibrational fields interacting with us. We are evolutionary beings that blend into the spaces where we spend time. This goes beyond the people that we spend time with—it is our internal ideas, beliefs, and thoughts.

If you find that the people in your tribe are not elevating you, then I encourage you to be open to letting other people into your ecosystem, or consider joining other unique ecosystems. Be intentional with who you would like to spend time with. What type of people are they? What goals do they have? How do they emotionally feel on average? What are their beliefs? Who do they look up to? Of course, you won't know everything about someone before meeting them.

I'm not encouraging you to interview people to be your friend. I am encouraging you to become hyper aware of who your ideal group of friends would be. Start allowing yourself to join online communities or Meet-Up get-togethers to rise out of your comfort zone and meet people who may align with your ideal tribe.

If you don't find people who inspire you, maybe you will inspire them? Who knows who you will meet that might help you with a project that you are working on, or might know someone who can help you. You may find that you are nervous or a little scared meeting new people, and that's normal.

Get out of your comfort zone and be better at connecting with new people. We can't change until we adapt our habits. We can't make new friends or relationships until we spend time and space around new people. This will bring in new perspectives, ways of thought, and new aspirations. This keeps a fresh outlook on life.

As we were getting closer and closer to meeting our baby, Greyson, the more excited I was feeling about the future of life's unknown. Everything felt new, and life was just beginning in every way. I felt so blessed. If you think about it, life is always starting at every single moment.

It was such an interesting introduction to Greyson. Greyson took 60 hours to transition into the world. He was comfortable in the womb, relaxed, and calm. But it was definitely not calm on the outside. It was scary as fuck. Anyone who has gone through having a baby knows what I'm talking about. A 60 hour labor is much longer than the norm. Barely having any sleep in that time, watching your partner go through intense and painful contractions, having nurses and doctors circulating in the room to update us with the labor process, without a doubt created immense stress.

I held my composure in the delivery room with my wife, but any time I had a moment to step outside, I would break down into tears. I had never been so scared. I wasn't sure if everything was okay. Maybe we were trying to force a natural birth when it just wasn't happening. I wasn't sure if our baby was going to make it, or what if my wife didn't make it through this experience?

The only person I could talk to was my mom. She held space for me and let me cry and express my fear. She prayed with me and gave me encouragement, like always. After ten minutes of giving myself permission to let go by releasing my fears, I would go back inside and refocus on making sure my wife felt supported. I didn't show any fear in the room. I only showed my strength. But I was a scared little boy underneath the shell.

At hour 40, my wife and I decided on an epidural. It wasn't part of our plan after doing months of research, but after that many hours, she was not dilated and totally exhausted from two days of contractions. She took the epidural and got some sleep. I couldn't sleep. I was on high alert, my thoughts were racing, and I was eager to get through this experience.

I spent my time meditating and praying while my wife slept. Funny things happen to your mind when you are sleep deprived, but I have had some pretty magical experiences during meditation.

This meditation specifically stands out in my mind as one of the most powerful and calming experiences of what would be a 60 hour labor. My eyes were closed, and I'm in a deep relaxed state. I'm asking God to show me what I need to see, to send angels, guides, and protectors to the hospital to watch over me, my wife, and Greyson. I prayed for the doctors and nurses. I finished the prayer part of my meditation and then dropped deeper into the listening part of my meditation.

What I saw was so surreal, so magical, and so perfect for what I needed. I saw globes of light everywhere, all different colors: purples, blues, green, yellows, oranges, and reds. It almost looked like bubbles were floating around and outside of the room. The energy I felt from these spheres of light radiated love, protection, safety, and gave me a sense of peace. Outside of the door, I saw the feet of giants and I could only see up to the ankles of these giants because the rest of them were beyond the ceiling of the hospital. There were seven giants guarding the outside of the room. I was told from that little whisper that the giants were here to guard us. They were around at all times, always protecting. They were here to ensure Greyson comes into the world safe, and that my wife will be safe. Whether my mind was playing tricks on me wasn't relevant. I felt an overwhelming amount of peace wash over me, and became confident in moving forward to the next morning.

Eight hours following that meditation, Greyson Wilder Dugan was born. It was the most impactful moment of my life, getting to see him come into this world, holding him against my chest, glaring deep into his eyes. I remember saying at that moment, "I missed you. You're finally here. I've been waiting for you my whole life."

It was such a crazy feeling to feel like I already knew Greyson from a long time ago. It felt like we were meeting again, not like it was our first meeting. I knew him forever, and now he's finally here. I missed him, and I felt as if his arrival made me whole. I instantly grew a foot taller. That moment changed me, and how I wanted to show up in the world. Life as I knew it would never be the same.

A chapter closed, and another one opened. Little did I know what type of transformation I would embark upon.

•

Three months after Greyson's birth, I made another hard decision.

I had clarity. I felt confident. I was in alignment with the bigger part of myself. I was getting ready to finish up a world-renowned coaching program. I just had my first baby (which definitely empowers you), and I was ready to do whatever it took to be an example for my son.

My wife and I had some challenges from the start of our relationship. We went through high and low waves as it goes in many relationships. The waves were intense, especially in the few years previous to our son arriving. At this point we have been together for ten years, and if I wrote the resume of the person who I wanted to be with, this woman met every criteria.

But we went through the same negative cycles. It seemed like no matter what we did, no matter how much we wanted things to work, we just couldn't get along for more than a week without fighting. From the outside, everything appeared perfect. We had built that perfect white picket fence family. Maybe what seems to be a reality from the outside is not the truth of how things are on the inside.

I can't speak for her and to respect her I won't go into much detail about our intimate relationship, but I would like to express some important points on this subject of marriage, as 50% end in divorce, including in the Christian communities, LGBTQ communities, inter-racial relationships, or however one identifies. Relationships are relationships are relationships. There are a lot of individuals that have challenges regarding intimate relationships. Here are a few areas that seem to come up with some of my clients, friends, and strangers.

- Not knowing what they want in a person

- Not able to find someone who they get along with

- Not knowing one's values

- Not knowing when to let go of relationships and when to move on

- Not knowing how to do the work, because the work, works

- Growing in different directions, or wanting different things out of life

- Staying together out of obligation rather than desire.

It's normal to have these feelings and experiences in a relationship. I believe that any relationship can work, but I'm not sure of the quality of relationship it will be if BOTH people aren't on board to engage in the sensitive and deep work of our inner worlds; such as childhood traumas, personality types, love languages, triggers, core fears, being creative in keeping the relationship fresh, keeping up with intimate sex, having open and honest communication, putting the needs of our partners first, and so on.

Relationships reveal our deepest internal insecurities and truths. I was the victim of my relationship.

Anyone that knows me would never label me a victim. They would think I was crazy for thinking so. I was, though, but not on purpose. I had valid reasons to feel this way, and however victimized we feel, it is our truth and it is absolutely valid. We may have a stockpile of reasons we feel our victimhood is valid, and will justify them with evidence after evidence, intending to prove to ourselves and everyone around us why it is true. This does not serve us, though. I believe we create our reality in two ways: Consciously and deliberately, or indeliberate without awareness.

I was an aware person back then, but there are layers of awareness. I needed more digging to understand who I was within relationships and what beliefs were driving my behaviors. If you are having challenges in your relationship, then I will say with confidence, it's your fault. I can feel you closing up after reading this.

You may think I don't know what type of relationship you're in, and you'd be right. I don't, but I know that everything in our life is our fault.

When we take ownership of everything that happens to us in our lives, we have the power. It seems extreme, but it's important that you do this for yourself, whether you're in an unhappy relationship and telling everyone you are happy, but truly, you are unfulfilled and wanting more. Or, you are doing all that you feel you can in your relationship, yet there are no changes.

You must be honest with yourself and your partner. Speak up about what's going right and what's going wrong in your relationship. I encourage you to work your ass off to make it work, no matter how hard it seems, or for you to stand up and say, "No more." If you remain in a relationship and you're unhappy, then that is your fault. You can either step your game up by doing the work showing vulnerability and letting down your guard, or you can step up by saying, "I can't do this anymore. This isn't working."

Being a victim is not an excuse to continue to live as a victim. Only you can make that change. Only you know what is or is not working for you, but you have to be completely honest by taking off the mask you've been wearing in your relationship. Yes, your partner might control, manipulate, abuse, is boring, has no ambition, is confrontational, might not care about anything, is void of passion, sucks with money, and might be way better than you in every way— it doesn't matter my friend, you chose them. Take accountability of your choice. Remain unhappy, or fix it.

Whatever question you have about your relationship, I can tell you now. You already know the answer. Are you willing to follow through on what you already know, or act like you don't know what step you must take next?

•

I knew what I needed to do for a long time. We were no longer on the same page and were growing in different directions. I had changed so much in the previous years and it caused unnecessary stress in our relationship. I felt I had to hold up the old version of myself before my transformation.

I could no longer wear this mask and couldn't take it off while I was in my marriage. I now know that this was a "me thing." She did her best to give me space to explore who I was in a time when I was lost, but I'm sure that it provided little comfort for her or the relationship, when the person she fell in love with was shifting into someone else.

•

I made the most challenging decision of my life just months after Greyson's birth. After a long and deep contemplation, I took courageous action to be on my own and restart my life. After 10 years together, we split up and then divorced.

It wasn't easy, but I knew what needed to be done. I always thought I was going to be the type of person who would be married forever, but after Greyson was born, something inside changed. If I wanted to be the man that I hoped to be for Greyson, I had to take this step.

My hopes of making this decision while he was only months old were so that he would never know his mom and I were together. He never would have a memory with us in a relationship, but always teammates, co-parenting in his best interest. I thought, maybe since we are both still young, we could find good, loving people that matched who we are. Maybe, just maybe, Greyson could have an example of what two healthy relationships look like? Perhaps he could have four conscious parents instead of two? I saw this as an opportunity to enhance each of our lives rather than creating something devastating.

I felt I had to make this decision now; for this to be a positive effect rather than a negative one, before he was old enough to form a memory of us together. I took a bold leap of faith and left the relationship.

Even though I believed that this was the right option, it completely terrified me. By choosing to leave my home, I was starting over. I gave my wife and our son the home we built together without asking for anything in return. I slept in my sister's home office on the floor for the next two months. Greyson would come over a few days a week as per our visitation agreement. He would never stay the night because he was still breastfeeding.

This was terribly hard on me. He slept on my chest almost every night of his first three months, and now? Nothing. Even with that challenge, I believed I was aligned and in flow, but after some time I questioned my decision to leave. I felt hurt. I felt guilty. I experienced shame.

No one understood the challenges we faced on the inside of our relationship, and I felt as if our friends and family were blaming me for leaving. In reality, in every relationship, there is a two-way street. I don't blame them though, I probably seemed crazy from everyone else's perspective. I left my ten-year relationship as soon as we had a child.

Greyson gave me clarity.

I found my worth when I met him. If he wasn't born, I might have remained in that relationship for years to come. He made me realize I needed to take immediate action.

But that decision took its toll. I would like to tell you that everything was peachy and perfect, but it wasn't. It was harder than I could have ever imagined. A piece of me died when I left, and it was the beginning of confronting my deepest shadows, the dark side of Jonathon, the part of me I had avoided my whole life.

I had no one else to blame if my life didn't work out how I had hoped.

It was time to face the reality of my insecurities and traumas.

PART 3

BECOMING NEW

CHAPTER 11
STARTING OVER

You would think that I was finally in a place where I could share what I had learned in the past handful of years. I had a long streak of transformational experiences where I was intentionally creating my life. I knew what I wanted. I was doing everything I could do to accomplish it. I was single, and no longer needed to consult with a partner about what I wanted to do or when I wanted to do it. I was free. I became a father, which was something that I had always wanted. I completed my coaching program and could finally do what I had hoped to do for a career.

Everything seemed to fall into place. But there was still a massive amount of internal work ahead of me. I wish I could say that I was open to doing that work during that time, but I would be lying. This was an extremely difficult time in my life.

I felt like a failure. Until this time in my life, I had won at everything; sports, finances, relationships, and life, but this time I had taken an enormous loss. At least that's how I perceived it, and if that is my perspective, then that is the reality I was experiencing. This toxic perspective of losing intertwined itself within my identity, and was affecting me to my core. I never tried at something as hard as I did with my marriage. I believe we both did. We went to counseling, read books, lowered our egos and learned how to communicate more effectively than we had ever done before, and we hoped we were going to make it work—out of sheer will, we would make it work! Yet, we failed, and we divorced.

Along with divorce came moments of shame, guilt, and regret. There was a period where I had to sit in that space in order to grieve. I had lost something I had worked hard for, and also the future idea of how I believed my life was supposed to be. Anyone who has experienced divorce understands how it feels. I believed starting over would be fun and exciting, but it turned out to be challenging, lonely, and daunting. I lost not only my wife but also my best friend.

I was sleeping on the floor of my sister's home. I only got to see my son three times a week. I was working full time, and I was attempting to start a business. I was going nonstop. Go. Go. Go. I didn't give myself permission to feel, or even take a breath. I was getting five hours of sleep at night. This type of lifestyle wasn't sustainable, but I hoped that I only had to do it for a short period, because after all, now that I'm Certified as a life coach, everyone will throw money at me, hoping I would coach them.

Obviously, that's not how it works. It can take years to build a successful practice, but for me, I had the belief that my entrepreneurial journey didn't have to be that way. I was different—clients would fall into my lap. I didn't know what I was doing. This was the first time I had ever been alone, and now I'm a father. I had never started a business before, and I didn't know the first step in creating a successful one. I already had paying clients by the time I graduated from my program, but it wasn't enough to supplement my six-figure income to support my lifestyle.

I placed an overwhelming amount of pressure on myself to force this coaching business to work, to force my life to work, to force myself to appear happy, as if everything was fine and dandy. In reality, I was experiencing false optimism. I was lying to myself so I could force myself to feel good, and not to feel any other emotions that didn't align with feeling good. This sounds familiar, right? I had done this my entire life. I blocked out all emotions that weren't positive, and just plastered a big smile on my face, while ultimately experiencing an internal void of all emotions. I was so stressed that I was finding coin size bald spots in the back of my scalp.

The brain is interesting. When it is under immense stress, it will trigger the fight-or-flight mechanism for protection, which is called your sympathetic state. I am one who experiences flight more than not. I'm actually a good fighter. It didn't matter if it was a physical fight, or a verbal confrontation, I would win; but I didn't like how fighting made me feel, or how I left the other person feeling in this scenario. So mostly I would lean toward the direction of flight.

Flight shows up outside of the assumed version of walking away from a stressful situation or experience. Sometimes it shows up as denial, numbing, avoiding, or distracting. Flight represents not owning up to the stress, not being honest about the stress, not dealing with the stress, or not sitting in the space to feel the stress. I did all the above, so that I didn't have to look at myself in the mirror to see what was really happening. Stress changes the brain, changes the lenses in how you see the world, and changes the way you engage in life with your behaviors.

I spent the next year distracting myself by grinding away in personal and business development, avoiding any negative emotions and trauma, numbing myself with sex, drugs, and alcohol, and denying any responsibility for the decisions that I had made with my finances, relationships, and life. I was living life full out in a sympathetic state of being, without even realizing how much stress was running through my life.

It took me four months to cry after splitting up with my wife. I got into a relationship as soon as my wife and I split. It wasn't supposed to be that way, but it just happened.

She was silly, conscious, and kind. She taught me so much about loving myself by the way she loved me. We connected deeply in a short period. She had a special gift, where she could heal those around her who felt alone or out of place. She created a space for them to feel loved and supported. This is what she did for me during a dark period in my life, and I will forever be grateful for the spirit she has, and how she kept me afloat when I could have easily sunk into a deep abyss.

The moment I allowed myself to feel what I was going through was a memorable one. I fasted for 48 hours. I was at the 24-hour point when I experienced pain, not just any pain, but extreme pain that I normally didn't experience during my fasts. My stomach hurt, my head was pounding, I felt drained, and I wanted to cry, but I couldn't. I had an energetic clog that needed to be purged from me. I've fasted for over 24 hours many times before, but this fast brought out more pain than I expected. If you are familiar with how energy works, then you know that when emotional blocks are ignored long enough, they will manifest themselves in physical dis-ease or pain.

Physical pain is energetic pain, depending on the emotional trauma happening in life for you. Again, I hadn't cried since leaving my wife after four months. I would not allow myself to cry or feel. It was more of a pride thing for me. Some of you might relate to this way of thinking. I have always felt as if I was good at suffering. I can endure a lot of pain. My ego would tell me I could handle anything that was thrown at me. I had a higher pain tolerance than anyone else. I was good at suffering.

This was the story running through my head because of my childhood trauma. I felt I turned out to be a pretty awesome adult, while keeping a smile on my face all along the way, so I was strong and I was good at suffering. What I didn't understand was that I was using a protective mechanism when around my family to feel safe. It worked, and it was actually serving me.

What happens when our protective mechanisms as children become outdated and no longer serve us as adults? It's simple. It harms us. We block out love, emotions, safety, trust, and just because the experience may look different on the outside, our internal process uses the same mechanism we used while we were experiencing our past traumas. We live an illusionary reality when our core beliefs are set within the framework of fear or trauma, and then the illusion becomes delusion.

We begin to lie to ourselves and justify why certain things keep happening to us. We believe that our own lies are the easiest lies to believe in, as we don't always question whether we are lying. We wouldn't lie to ourselves; would we? We lie to ourselves more than we think. This is how we live in the same cycles without taking ownership of our own reality. We blame the outside world for our problems, which is understandable, but at what point do we take responsibility for our present and future experiences? If we don't notice the cycles, then we will never be the creator of our reality, but reality would be our creator. That's the difference between creating by default, and creating with deliberate intent.

Back to this period of fasting. The person I was dating was so loving and caring to me that while I was away from my apartment taking my son back to his mother, she hand wrote and posted close to 50 affirmation little sticky notes around my apartment. Here are some examples: "I am a powerful creator." "I am loved." "I can do this." "I'm strong." "I am worthy." "I deserve love." "I am forgiven." "Everything is gonna be OK." "This too shall pass." "I can do anything." "I possess so much magic inside of me." "I am meant to be seen." "I am meant to be loved." "I am healing." "I'm safe to feel." "I am made of stardust."

When I walked into the apartment and saw this, I fell to my knees and broke down sobbing.

I hadn't shed a tear in over four months. I had bottled everything up until the point of explosion. I was like a champagne bottle that had been shaken up, and these sticky notes allowed my cork to pop. Before this moment, I didn't want to feel anything.

When you block off negative emotion, you block off positive emotion. Emotion is emotion to the universe, and it's our body's way to communicate. When we block it off, or numb emotion, then we lose the communication.

Finally, I could let go.

I didn't have to be strong anymore. I was carrying around so much weight, so much guilt, so much shame, and so much pressure. I surrendered down on my knees and gave it all away; away to who? I don't know—just away. It wasn't my burden to carry any longer. I felt release. I felt lighter. I was healing at that moment.

After 20 minutes, I pulled myself together, and I sat in my room to meditate for the next hour. I sat there, allowing myself the space to feel, feel without judgement. Feel to just feel, without trying to fix anything, no matter how much it scares me I need to spend time with myself by myself.

Sometimes we just need a best friend when we are at our lowest of lows, and sometimes the best friend to have in those moments is you—if we are open and brave enough to allow it.

Following the meditation, the physical pain I was experiencing just hours earlier no longer existed. I didn't feel any emotional pain, or spiritual pain. I felt more connected and like myself than I had felt for a long time. I was almost high because of all the heavy energy I had released. I felt as if I was floating in a cloud of self-love and joy. I learned the powerful "medicine" of fasting during that 48-hour period. It makes sense why fasting is a tool in every spiritual text from the beginning of time.

•

I would love to tell you that after that experience, everything turned up, and that I felt better, getting my life back into order, but I could only hold that bliss for a short period. I fell back into the same cycle again, and again, and again. I was still broken. I was doing the best that I knew how, but my best was not working. Every time I stood up, I fell back down. I drank most days of the week, along with smoking weed. The new relationship ended with no fault to her. I didn't know how I wanted to move forward in my business.

I was always so tired. I felt as if I didn't have any energy for myself. I was giving it to my newborn, my full-time job, my business, partying, and left nothing for taking care of myself with love. I can clearly see in hindsight, that I was nowhere close to loving myself, but in fact hating myself. Consciously, no, I didn't hate myself, but the way I treated my mind, body, emotions, and soul was not how someone who loves themselves would treat themselves.

CHAPTER 12
THE SHIFT

After months of self-destruction, something finally shifted. Perhaps it was time healing me, or the internal work I was making a priority was actually working, or I was sick and tired of self-sabotaging? I would guess it was a combination.

I was feeling I had room to breathe.

When energy shifts, you'll notice life parallels your energetic shift. When I least expected it, I met someone. I have been working with Mackenna for years, but we had never had a conversation. The unfortunate truth about this woman was that she didn't even know my name. It's a funny story, or maybe an embarrassing story, but I would like to share it with you.

We both worked at Gordon Ramsay Steak. You know, that famous chef that yells at everyone on TV? He's actually one of the kindest people I've ever met, but his TV persona is pretty intense.

One day, Mackenna and I were standing at the well in front of the bar where servers and cocktail servers wait for their guest's drinks to be made by the bartender. For years we shared this space, and we didn't talk. We were friendly to each other without engaging. I look back in appreciation. I was married for most of that time and she was with someone, so that showed me we were both faithful in our relationships.

I had been single for a little while at this point and my eyes were opening to new opportunities. I was reaching for one of my drinks and simply asked how she was doing, and when I talk to fellow co-workers, I call them by name because that's what I had always done, it's a sign of respect. When I called her by her name, I noticed she avoided saying my name. I didn't think too far into it, and asked questions about her life. She talked about her dog, her cats, and how she was looking for a new job. It was a surface level conversation as we had little time to go deeper on anything since we were working.

The next day I did the same thing, "Hey Mackenna, how are you today?" She said, "Good, hooow arrre you?" I knew at that moment that she wasn't sure about my name.

So I did what any guy would do. I smiled and followed up with, "What's my name, Mackenna?" I called her out, which I wouldn't normally do, but we had been working together for two years. Not that big of a restaurant to not know everyone's name.

Slightly embarrassed, she softly answered, "I'm sorry, I don't know."

I chuckled and smiled, "Two years and you don't know my name? I must not be very memorable, huh? Well, my name is Jonathon. It's nice to re-meet you, Mackenna."

The funny thing is, the next day I saw her, she was so eager to run into me so that she could say my name, "Hi, John. How are you today?"

I laughed to myself and asked her, "John? Who's John? My name is Jonathon."

I told her how I didn't go by John, as that was my father's name. I didn't care to hear people call me John. It was Jonathon, or Dugan, but not John.

Again, she was embarrassed, but we laughed about it. It was a running joke for the next few months. Eventually, she asked me if I wanted to have a drink after work one night, and we connected. We started dating. We were right in front of each other for two years before we even noticed each other, yet when we finally did, we were inseparable.

Mackenna was different. We surrounded our relationship with fun. There was no pressure. I made my intentions clear, as she also made her intentions clear. We both had gotten out of relationships and we needed to work on ourselves. We held each other accountable to that. She was a free spirit, full of love and compassion. We always had a great time together. She was full of mystery, yet so magical. We based most of our conversations on spirituality and personal growth and development. We never argued, we never fought; we hung out enjoying excellent dinners and delicious wine while laughing.

Even though we had a healthy relationship, I didn't want to be in one. I had trauma around my last relationship and I felt jaded. I kept telling myself that I needed to be alone, but how can I pass up this opportunity? She's everything I had always asked for. So, we continued to hang out until love crept in and made space in our hearts. I'm sure I had something to do with it, but I believe Greyson took a big role.

I remember the first time she visited Greyson. Mackenna was bouncing a ping-pong ball down on the ground and making a PEW sound, and Greyson couldn't stop laughing. It was the funniest thing he had ever experienced. He was barely over one-year-old, and learning how to walk. He was laughing so hard that he could hardly stay standing. I believe that's when Mackenna fell in love, not only with me but also with Greyson Wilder. They have been best friends ever since.

•

As Mackenna and I continued to grow our relationship, I was working intensely on my coaching business, High-Conscious Living. I created a program called *Transform Your Life In 100 Days*. I was gaining clients, challenging myself on camera, and getting into the best shape of my life through eating healthy, doing yoga, running, and body weight exercises. This differed from my heavy weightlifting; force feeding myself and taking weight gainers to increase weight through muscle mass. It was never sustainable, as I'm the type of person who loses weight if I'm not constantly working out or eating a lot.

I had created a routine that served the lifestyle I was yearning to live. I had to change my mindset, my beliefs, and my daily actions. One belief I took on was from a quote by American author Annie Dillard, "How you live your days, is of course, how you live your life."

I structured my days in ways where it was full of healing, awareness, presence, creation, and execution. My days were intentional in creating the version of myself I had visualized for my future ideal self. This future ideal self was my hero, and I looked upon him constantly to show me my path.

This is what an average day looks like when I have a full day. I wake up at 7 a.m., meditate and exercise, journal and attend coaching calls. By ten, I'd pick up Greyson, and he stayed with me until three. I was intermittent fasting, so I would eat my first meal with Greyson at noon. Work takes up the time from 4 p.m. to midnight. By two in the morning, after another round of yoga, meditation and journaling, I go to bed.

I did this for 200 days as part of my Transform Your Life in 100 Days program. If I was going to coach anyone through this program, then I better be living it out. I also learned how to play guitar in this time, and basic Spanish, as these were a few of my 100 day goals.

There were days where I didn't follow through. Sometimes I would get off track for a week at a time, but I never gave up. I practiced perseverance and resilience by starting over each time I strayed from my routine. My life was moving in a positive direction. There were a few faults in my routine, though. I didn't schedule any intentional time for fun and enjoyment. I was sleep deprived. I didn't make time for my relationship, and I was constantly on the verge of a burnout.

I needed to speak with my life coach and good friend, Eduardo Crespo.

I sat down for breakfast one morning with Eduardo, and I told him about everything I was working on, and how much I was accomplishing in my business and personal life. I also told him I felt as if something was missing. I felt I wasn't being fulfilled in my work. I was unhappy, because all I was doing was working and accomplishing. I still wasn't able to leave my evening job. My coaching practice wasn't making the money I needed to supplement that income.

He asked me if I took any days off. I laughed and told him I had one day a week to myself where I didn't have to go to my day job or have Greyson. I spent the entire day working on my business. I loved working on my business. It didn't feel like work to me. It was freeing. I was exercising my passion, and I was doing work that brought value to others. I wished I had more days where I could completely get lost in my work.

Eduardo probed deeper, and asked, "Well, what would it look like if you took one full day for yourself each week, not working on your business, not running errands, and not working out? What if you took a day off from doing, and you allowed yourself to rest by being?"

I became uncomfortable with that question and rambled off all the reasons it wasn't possible. "That's my only day to get into flow and work. That is a day off for me, because I love what I do. I have too much to do, to take a day off. I want to get out of my night job so that I can do what I love every day and have a free schedule to spend more time with Greyson."

As I continued to make excuses, I noticed how I'm reacting and how my coach was smiling. Eduardo gave me space to finish speaking and replied to my answer with, "Your response is interesting, Jonathon. I never said you have to take a day off. This was only a hypothetical question. Why do you think it makes you uncomfortable to take a day off?"

I sat in silence for a moment then energy broke away from me. I got emotional and shed a few tears. He broke the silence, emphatically saying, "It seems as if you are more comfortable doing, rather than being. What do you think about that?"

Fuck, that hit me hard. At that moment, I realized I was in the same cycle that I had put myself in time and time again, but now wearing a different mask. I had filled my addiction up with accomplishing, personal development, coaching, and was not giving myself the space to feel how I was feeling, or the time I needed to love myself. It burned me out because I wasn't taking care of myself. Even though I was doing good work, I was distracting myself from being present with myself. What I needed was my best friend. ME.

From that day on, I scratched out everything I was working on in that year and started over. Of course, we are never starting over. We have new perspectives, more knowledge, new awareness, and hopefully some fresh wisdom. Goodbye 2019 and hello 2020.

CHAPTER 13
SEEING CLEARLY
WITH 2020 VISION

I released this book at the end of 2021, and depending on when you are reading it, you may or may not know about 2020. The beginning of the year was amazing. It started out productive. The economy was at a high and momentum was on my side. I always created a little mantra at the start of each year to keep my mind focused on my intention.

This year I repeated, "Take off my mask and put on my cape." It was all about letting go of all my false identities, the old me, and becoming the hero in my life by stepping into my ultimate power.

In the first two months of 2020, I moved into a new home. I went through a Theta Healing workshop. I got my finances in order. I went to Phoenix to see Tom Bilyeu. I experienced breathing exercises and cold exposure in a Wim Hof workshop; witnessed the Grand Canyon for the first time, and experienced my first professional baseball and basketball game. I was leading monthly hikes, working with many clients, volunteering, and my personal relationships were thriving. This was going to be the best year yet. This is the year.

Then on Greyson's birthday, March 17th, 2020, the Las Vegas strip shut down. The entire world shut down. The coronavirus, COVID-19, took hold and changed the landscape of how the world lived. There was mass hysteria everywhere. The grocery stores ran out of food, millions lost their jobs, including myself, face masks were being mandated across the globe. Sports shut down and were no longer on TV. People were getting sick or dying, and people across America were running out of toilet paper. This was such a memorable year never experienced in the history of our existence.

People around the world were sharing in the same experiences, regardless of race, religion, gender, age, social status, or sexual preferences. We were all at war with a virus. Consciousness was shifting on a grand scale, and at a rapid rate.

It wasn't all bad. I did dive deep down into the rabbit holes of conspiracy theories, which fucked me up a bit. It was an election year and I believe that there was a mass agenda behind the scenes of the media that was being pushed down our throats. There was a civil war that was being encouraged between blacks and whites, democrats and republicans, mask wearers vs. non-mask wearers, pro-vaccines against non-vaccines, this science vs. that science, is it for our safety or are we being controlled, and the divisional lists go on and on.

I saw life more clearly. I learned a lot about myself. I didn't work for a full year, so it gave me space and time to spend on myself, family, and my coaching practice. Mackenna and I moved in together and that taught us a lot about our relationship. I could have dinner at home every night, which I hadn't been able to do because of years of working night shifts. I spent so much quality time with Greyson and the people who mattered the most. I learned I held most of my security and safety based on the external, and as soon as everything was flipped upside down with COVID-19, that safety didn't exist until I forced myself to go inside myself to find it again. I created deep intentional friendships with people around the country and up in Canada, using Zoom.

We called ourselves The Surrender Crew. I have never had a group of people where we could share deep and meaningful growth together. I went deeper into my meditation practice by becoming certified as an instructor, and by creating a free beginner's meditation course.

I finally, for the first time in my life, didn't have to go to work. I could rest and heal my past trauma. I went to sleep at nine every night and woke up at five. I never thought I was a morning person until I experienced being a morning person. I got clear on my goals, and created a new business, A Hero's Academy. I experimented with a podcast, Moments of AHA! This was where I interviewed everyday heroes and asked them how they became the hero in their lives, while also giving weekly tips on how to improve people's lifestyles. 2020 had its waves for sure, but I was still accomplishing so much. With all the growth I had experienced that year, I also slowly fell back into familiar patterns.

When quarantine started, I drank almost every day. Did I get drunk every day? No, but I had one or two glasses of wine every day. Once a week three to four glasses of wine, but hey, I was still accomplishing so many things, and I was waking up early. Why did it matter that I created this habit?

This habit had crept in slowly, and it replaced the time that I made during my meditations to self reflect, to now, reflecting at the end of the night with a glass of wine and a joint. It was an interesting irony that as soon as I got certified as a meditation instructor, I stopped meditating. I again distracted myself with doing and accomplishing, rather than being. This was having a negative effect on my emotional state, and transferred into my relationship with Mackenna.

During quarantine, Mackenna took advantage of this time and received her 200-hour Yoga certification after already being certified in Trauma Recovery Yoga and in Kids Yoga. This was a perfect compliment to the holistic coaching and education I wanted to bring to people through A Hero's Academy, so we worked on the business together. Nothing could go wrong. We were the perfect duo to accomplish such dreams.

Well, I've been wrong once or twice in my life. We weren't ready to step into business together. We no longer had a fun, free, and playful relationship. I love what I do. I love learning about business, coaching, and working hard for long hours. It's fun. But not everyone sees entrepreneurship in that same light. I have been developing this practice for years, so when Mackenna jumped in, it was overwhelming for her. I added more and more work and pressure on her, while she wanted to enjoy teaching and yoga. The business bled into our relationship, and as our teamwork dwindled, so did our relationship.

Mackenna is a kind and caring soul, so rather than being honest about how she felt about our partnership in the business, and how she wasn't having fun anymore in our relationship, she held it all inside. She closed up and became distant. She knew how important my business was to me, as I believed that the information that we processed in changing the direction of our lives could also change other people's lives for the better. I didn't do it for the money. I wasn't making money at my coaching because I took a break from taking on clients to restructure my goals and the direction of the business. So could you even call A Hero's Academy a business? Maybe an obsessive hobby or passion? That's probably more accurate. Either way, she felt like it would have crushed me if she told me the truth, so she closed herself off, and I was getting frustrated with the lack of connection.

The following morning, after a weekend binge drinking from Halloween, I woke up out of a deep sleep to an overwhelming amount of guilt and shame. I felt like my head might rip open if I even sniffled my nose, and the subtlest movement of my body could cause me to erupt in vomiting. My hangover was horrendous.

At that moment, a voice from within me said, "No more, Jonathon. You can't keep doing this to yourself." I'm sure everyone in the history of time has had that same voice tell them this when waking up with a hangover. We reply with, "I'll never drink this much again." Then, a week or two later, we find ourselves in the same position.

I tend to be light on myself when I make mistakes. Guilt and shame can crush the soul of any person. I gently told myself, "It's okay. I need to forgive myself, and move on."

Usually that worked, but this time that inner voice spoke up. "Forgive yourself for what? Why should you forgive yourself when you haven't said sorry? Not only that, you haven't said sorry for anything specific. If you were going to ask for forgiveness from someone that you cared about, someone that you loved, then you would be specific about your apology, and then make sure you wouldn't do it again. If you didn't care about the person who you said sorry to, then you would repeat the same mistakes with no remorse. To me, it doesn't seem like you LOVE yourself, but it does seem like you HATE yourself. If you love yourself, then you would treat your mind better. If you love yourself, then you would treat your body better. If you love yourself, then you would honor your soul better. You may lie to Jonathon, but you can't lie to me. So if you want to forgive yourself, tell yourself sorry, and be specific about what you are apologizing for. Do this as if you were speaking to someone that you love and care about."

Fuck, that hit home. Tears rolled down my cheeks as the truth resonated all throughout this conversation. I was reflecting on how I had been treating myself. I thought that if I were in a relationship with myself, what would I say? Would I feel loved? Would I feel wanted? The answer was a definite, "HELL NO." I was not treating myself with love. My inner voice was right. It seemed like I actually hated myself.

I followed the instructions of my inner voice, and went down a list of things I wanted to apologize for while speaking to myself in the third person; as if I was talking to someone I deeply cared about. Funny thing was, I might have spoken to myself in the third person, but as soon as my heart opened up, my inner voice stepped in to take the lead.

"Jonathon, I'm so sorry for treating you like shit lately. Jonathon, I'm sorry that you feel you have to drink to numb your pain. Jonathon, I'm sorry that you feel lost and confused right now. Jonathon, I'm sorry that you feel so alone. Jonathon, I'm sorry that you are working your ass off and not getting the results that you were hoping for. Jonathon, I'm sorry that your best friend had to die. I know that wasn't easy on you. Jonathon, I'm sorry you haven't been the same ever since. Jonathon, I'm sorry all of this feels hard and heavy for you to carry alone. Jonathon, I'm sorry that your marriage ended. That has definitely taken a toll on you as well. Jonathon, I'm sorry you had to start over after building a beautiful home. Jonathon, I'm sorry it's been difficult being a single dad for the last two years. Jonathon, I'm sorry you lost your job. Jonathon, I'm sorry that you got into debt, and the weight of $60k is crushing you. Jonathon, I'm sorry that you can't look at yourself in the mirror, because you are afraid of what you might see. Jonathon, I'm sorry. I'm sorry. I'm sorry. The truth is, Jonathon, I love you. The truth is that I am here for you. I have been here since the beginning, every step of the way. The truth is that you are not alone. I have always been with you. You have to be open to receiving help. I am your best friend, but you have to allow me to be that for you, and you have to be that for me. The truth is that I don't forgive you, because there is nothing to forgive. Everything that you have ever gone through has led to this moment. It's perfection. The truth is that I am the Inner Hero. The truth is; I Am. I am Jonathon, and you are Jonathon, and we are the great I Am. It's time to align with me. I have forgiven you since the beginning. Now it's time for you to forgive yourself, as YOU are the only thing getting in the way from US becoming ONE. Self-love is the work, and the only work that matters."

I'm completely sobbing. I haven't allowed myself to feel how hard life has been for me in the last few years. I would never acknowledge and validate where I was. I kept my head down and worked my ass off.

It obviously wasn't working. I was on a hamster wheel, sprinting faster and faster while not progressing, at least not where it counted. I felt like the snake that was eating its own tail.

I knew I had to change something. I could see with 20/20 vision what my life had become when I wasn't loving myself. I could no longer carry around this guilt. I could no longer carry around this shame. I want to move forward, toward self-love.

CHAPTER 14
THERE IS NO BOTTOM TO THE ABYSS

I thought I had hit my rock bottom. I thought that countless times in the past, but somehow the universe is laughing at me, saying, "There is no bottom to the abyss, as there is no ceiling to the heavens."

I took responsibility for my substance abuse and my self-hate, following the morning when my Inner Hero spoke to me. I stopped drinking and smoking weed for one month. I focused on work instead. If my urge to drink were overwhelming, I would head to the gym.

My brain was shifting. It takes anywhere from seven to ten days for alcohol to leave the brain, sometimes longer depending on how much one partakes. Anyone who knows about the brain knows that after consuming alcohol and marijuana for nine months straight, five nights a week, it's going to take a toll on your energy and your emotional state.

My body was affected, and with some of those changes came irritability. I was triggered more than normal. So when Mackenna wasn't following through or she was no longer feeding the business with the creative ideas that were once exciting for her; and regarding our relationship, unless she was drinking, she avoided talking to me. I felt overwhelmed and took everything personally.

A wedge had taken form over those months and it was rapidly spreading us further apart. Since I was no longer numbing by drinking and smoking, I was experiencing the unsettled resentment. One night at dinner, she was honest about her feelings. This was our first date night since I had stopped drinking, but this night I was going to allow myself a few drinks. We needed a night alone, so that we could reconnect. The dinner was going great at first, but she had intentions for a more serious conversation.

As soon as she had a few glasses of Champagne, she gained the courage she needed to speak. She felt as if she wasn't a priority in my life, and asked where she stood on my list of priorities.

I didn't have her high on that list at that moment, and her question irritated me. Like I said, it easily triggered me, as my brain and body were undergoing these changes. Plus, I felt like we were going to reconnect and have a nice date night at a fine dining steak house, with some delicious Napa Valley Cabernet Sauvignon. I had been saving this wine for the past five years. I was looking forward to enjoying this after a month of cleansing and taking a break from any substances, then perhaps going home to connect intimately, but instead we were having this serious conversation.

My list of priorities is:

1. Me and my health. I needed to get my shit together by making my mental, physical, and spiritual health number one.

2. Greyson. Being a great dad has always been towards the top of this list!

3. My business (where I wasn't making money), but it was my passion and what I felt to be my life's purpose.

4. Mackenna, and our relationship. I loved her, but she came after my first three priorities.

Obviously, you don't have to be a rocket scientist to know that wasn't the answer she wanted. No one wants to be number four on a list of priorities. I was saying, if I had any extra time, then she could have it. She didn't want to be the leftovers, or be an afterthought, but to be a priority. She wasn't asking to be number one, nor was she asking me to push my passions off to the side, or that she had to be more important than Greyson. She needed commitment and to be wanted. Mackenna wanted to have more kids and to get married at some point. Not now, or soon, but that was what she wanted. She wanted to know that we were going to have a future together, and for me, I wasn't sure if that's what I wanted. I thought maybe I could want that later, but as far as that moment went, I was happy with where we were. That was a lie. Neither of us was happy with where we were, and that's why we had that conversation.

•

When I was certified as a meditation instructor, I stopped meditating. I would do maybe 10 to 15 minutes a week, if that. I was drinking a lot, and working 12 hour days on A Hero's Academy, creating content, a YouTube Channel, interviews, and creating an online course. How did this happen again? I was ignoring myself, and what I needed, AGAIN.

I slowly fell back into fight or flight. It had been subtly creeping in for months with no awareness. Yes, I took some responsibility for my drinking and smoking, but substances were only one aspect of dealing with stress.

The false optimism, numbing with alcohol and marijuana, and avoiding what was helping in the past—meditating, journaling, exercising—returned to haunt me. Mackenna? Same pattern. I'm proud of Mackenna for recognizing that something was off with us, and for her to stand up for what she wanted in our relationship. She knew what her value was worth.

The next day, she left me.

No other conversation, no closure, no how do we make this work, nothing. She said she was packing up her belongings and leaving. She told me she deserved more than what she was receiving, and she was right. Flight took place, and it left me in the dust to figure out my shit by myself.

Her decision blindsided me, even though in hindsight, everything added up. I wanted us to figure out how to make things work between us, but I wasn't ready. I wasn't open to change. I was completely closed off, detached from reality, and obsessed with a business that didn't make money. I blamed her for why we didn't succeed in our relationship, and she blamed me. We were in each other's mirror, yet we didn't want to see the lessons. Her leaving me at one of my low points was a blessing in disguise.

I was already at my annual burnout stage. Well, at least that's what I believe it was, combined with seasonal depression. Every year around the same time Michael died, I went into a downward spiral of depression and burnout. This was the fourth year in a row, and now I understand why this was happening. I overloaded my schedule and tasks for 10 months straight, and didn't take a season of rest and reflection until the universe forced it on me.

For the next few months, I felt broken more than I had ever felt. I had a tough time after my divorce, but I never allowed myself to feel it. This time, I was feeling all of it. I was amid my first broken heart. I don't know why it's called a broken heart when the pain comes in the pit of my solar plexus. I was walking around feeling as if I had a thousand pounds of rocks resting in my gut. I couldn't eat, and I felt like I was going to throw up every few hours. This wasn't the only area where I was feeling like shit.

Since I still wasn't drinking, the entire unresolved trauma I hadn't healed came to a head. I couldn't blame anyone else for where I was. No one was around to blame, only me. I was the common thread in these broken experiences.

This brought me to another one of those, Moments of AHA! I couldn't avoid myself any longer. It was time to confront my inner darkness, my inner fear, my self-sabotage, and my self-hate. If I continued moving forward in this space, everything that I had built for myself would crumble and fall. There was no way I was going to let that happen.

CHAPTER 15
TIME TO SURRENDER

There are lessons in the abyss—if we open our eyes, our ears and our hearts. We must realize our core beliefs. Our core beliefs are driving the results we manifest. What are my core beliefs in my life? Not what I want my core beliefs to be or what I THOUGHT they were, but what core beliefs were leading to my current results, and why? Here is a sequence of questions that I asked myself to understand what paradigms were driving my results. You must look at your life objectively and be radically honest.

What are my results? Why am I doing this? Why don't I deserve love and success? Why do I have to live alone? Create an exhaustive list. Write as much as you can. Be honest. Do the work, because the work, works.

This exercise brought me a ton of awareness. I understood why I had manifested the results I had in my life. Out of fear, I created my ultimate hell. I was in a prison of self-sabotage. Without awareness, nothing can ever change. Awareness is the first step in knowing what you would like to transform in your life. It is the key to the prison I had manifested for myself.

The bible says, "As on Earth as it is in Heaven." This means that we can attain Heaven, or Christ Consciousness right now, in this moment, while we are in the physical realm.

The same goes for, "As on Earth as it is in Hell." We can also manifest a consciousness of darkness, suffering, and doom. We can experience Hell, here on the physical plain, just as we can experience Heaven. Awareness of knowing where you are located, and having clarity in where you would like to be, can give you the opportunity to redirect your path along your journey. You must find awareness through being honest with yourself, and shining light in all the dark corners of your soul.

I found where I was located regarding my core beliefs. Now, I had to become clear about where I truly wanted to be, and ask myself if I'm WILLING to do and be what it takes to get there.

Some beliefs I discovered through this process was that I wanted to remarry, and have more children. I wanted to love myself, bring value to everyone around me, focus energy in one space at a time, trust in the process; the universe is always at work for my highest good.

By being clear about what I really wanted and the beliefs I had around what I wanted, made me understand how much healing I needed. After my divorce, I said that I would never put a relationship over my passion. I didn't create that belief out of being conscious, but out of hurt and pain.

I said that I didn't know if I would ever want to get married again, because I ruined the sacred communion of marriage after my divorce. I thought it meant nothing anymore, but I was wrong. I said that out of resentment and being jaded. I said that I wasn't sure if I wanted more kids, because I wanted to accomplish so many things before having another one.

In reality, I'll always want to accomplish things, and that won't go away if I have more kids. I love being a father. I told myself that I could do everything and anything, but that led to burnout and incremental progress.

I would talk about how all I wanted to do was to be happy, yet I pushed away all the things that made me happy. The list goes on and on with understanding the contradictions in the vibrational reality that I was experiencing, compared to the vibrational reality I desired. It just didn't match. I was self-sabotaging, and it was time to get the fuck out of my way.

I was in a place where I humbled myself to the lessons of the abyss. I was not the perfect person I was trying to hold myself to. I would tell people all the time, "No one is perfect. As in, not one person in this entire universe is perfect and in that, is perfection."

Even though I had said this for years, I didn't believe it applied to me. I thought I had to be an example of perfection. With a belief like that, no wonder I kept failing. Perhaps the belief that I should have been having is to BE the example of the uniqueness of what I am? There is perfection in the journey of who I am. There is only one, I Am, and that is I, me, Jonathon Calhoun Dugan. I am unlike anyone else in the universe, a unique drop in the ocean, yet I am the same as you, a drop in the ocean. I am part of the whole, the ocean of existence, which means I am the ocean—the whole. I Am.

I was shedding a lot of energy in this period after Mackenna and I split up, just as leaves fall from the trees during fall, or the snake's skin peels from its body to grow. I was hurting. Energy work can be hard sometimes. I didn't want to look in the mirror and take complete ownership of my reality, but I knew I had to if I wanted to move forward in my life's purpose, or even if I just wanted to live a loving and happy life.

I hiked three times a week, meditated daily, and took Epsom salt baths every night before bed. I was journaling again for the first time in months, and taking my workouts more seriously, as this was one of my ways to express anger and frustration healthily. I returned to the basics. This was the foundation of my transformation years earlier. The most important thing I did though, was not what I was doing externally; it was a choice I made in my heart, and that was to surrender to how I thought things had to go for my happiness, for my success, and for my impact on the world. It all means nothing if I'm alone and feeling burdened by all the self-imposed weight. It was time to let go.

Within just a few weeks of deciding to let go of my ego, and to let go of all the plans I had for my business, I still felt heavy. I needed a reset. I needed to get away. I didn't have time to grieve for Mackenna. I was working again in the restaurant and when I wasn't, I was with Greyson.

Any parent knows it takes a lot of focus and attention to raise a toddler, especially if you are doing it by yourself. I had been doing this since he was three months old. Greyson's mom is amazing. She's such an exemplary mother. We co-parent well together and it's the best we have ever got along, now that we weren't together. We split time with Greyson almost 50/50.

In the last year, Mackenna also had a significant role in Greyson's life. They loved each other, and she treated him as her own. They met right before his first birthday. He's never known me with anyone else. She's his "M." That's what he would call her, or "Mock-N-na." Now that she's gone, I was doing it alone, again.

Despite everything that I had gone through in the last few years, Greyson wasn't negatively affected. Not just because he was a baby, but also because I didn't show him that side. The only thing he knows is the energy I projected toward him. I projected and showered him with love, patience, presence, and affection. He is the happiest little boy you will ever meet. He is so full of love and light. Not only does he have the biggest little heart, he is a borderline genius. You might think that every parent thinks this about their child, and maybe you're right, but I believe he is special. He has a photographic memory, reads books, knows his planets in order, counts to 120, understands math, and is a master of the 50 piece puzzle; at only three-years-old.

I have to tell you a bit more about this precious little boy. He brings me so much joy. On his third birthday, we held a space birthday party. He received an overwhelming amount of presents. This could have been the best day of his life. After every present, before he would open the next present, he would go to the person who gave it to him, and would say thank you, and give a big hug. Every. Single. Present. It was so sweet to observe how he made other people feel appreciated and special.

That night when it was time for him to go to bed, he kept coming out of his room and would stand at the top of the staircase, which is unusual for him. After the third time, I went into his room with him and asked if everything was okay. He was laying his head on his pillow, looking at me with big watery eyes, and with his broken toddler language said, "Pushed Avi-nona on trampoline." Being as sincere as I could, I repeated back to him, "You pushed Aviana on the trampoline?"

He continued, "Yeeahhh. Hurt Avi-nona on trampoline."

I looked at him with compassion as he was talking about one of his friends. I nodded my head and repeated what he had just told me. "You did? You hurt Aviana when you pushed her on the trampoline? Did you get to say sorry?"

Watching his little brain work, he looked down, then back up at me, "No. Sorry Avi-nona."

I watched as his energy shifted in that moment and let him keep reflecting on his day, "Thank you da-yee for helping open presents for you."

I smiled and laughed, as what he meant to say was, "Thank you daddy for helping me open presents." He is still working on it.

He continued to reflect on his day and all the fun experiences with his friends. When he was done, he told me he loved me and said goodnight. Now he was ready for bed. I left his bedroom feeling so much love and appreciation.

He had reflected on his day by not only giving gratitude for what he had experienced, but he also didn't want to go to bed with a guilty conscience. At three, he has already developed emotional intelligence and awareness. This makes me more proud of him than his ability to do puzzles, count, do math, or read. He is conscious, and consciousness flows through him. It's amazing, and he teaches me so much about myself, along with life every day.

So while Greyson is with me, I am present and remove all the other worries and distractions in life. I don't work on my coaching business, or read or write. I don't go on the computer or my phone to check social media. Well, maybe I check it, but I don't get absorbed into my phone for hours at a time. I'm present.

I don't allow myself to feel what I'm feeling, but push it to the side. I'm still working on getting better at showing him all sides of me. It will assist him as a healthy example for when he is feeling an array of emotions.

Greyson didn't understand what was going on after Mackenna left. He would ask about her every time he came over, "Where's Mock-N-na?" It made my heart ache even more than it already did. "She's at Megan's buddy. She's going to stay over there now." Without skipping a beat, he would say, "Oh. She's at Me-gans." The one place I could usually escape, where I could be ultimately present, forgetting about the outside world and problems that I was facing, was no longer available. Even with him, it reminded me of my broken heart.

All I knew was that I needed to get away, and fast. I needed a break. I needed a reset. I wanted to go on a retreat somewhere, but where could I go? It was December 2020. There were no gatherings. There were no retreats because of COVID-19. Until I saw that a friend on Facebook was hosting an event the following weekend in Venice Beach, CA with Humans I Trust. I didn't have the money to be spending, but I decided $1000 for a 12-hour workshop with Spiritual Entrepreneurs is worth the investment, if I can get away and find some sort of clarity and healing.

CHAPTER 16
I'M A DREAMER

As soon as I decided to attend the workshop, the money that I needed came to me instantly, and that same night I had a dream—a powerful dream; it was so vivid, so real. Every once in a while, I would have such dreams. These dreams wouldn't come to me while I was sleeping, but during my meditations, which could be called my visions. Other times, rather than visions, I would receive whispers that were extremely clear and direct.

There's an internal voice or guidance that speaks to us and shows up with what we need to know. We all have these interesting gifts. It doesn't matter whether it's God or the universe talking to us, or if it's our subconscious releasing energy, this is how we try to interpret or make sense of it. In reality, it's happening, and being experienced through us. So, if we are experiencing it, then it is based on the lenses of our perceptive reality.

What I found on my journey is that what matters is that our brain has control of our body and our experiences. With the placebo, as an example, by believing in something and convincing ourselves of any reality that we put energy into, our body will respond in congruence to the amount of faith and knowing that we have about a specific reality, adding evidence to the phrase, "Thoughts create our reality." This belief expands toward health or sickness, love or hate, abundance or lack, wealth or poverty, whether you can or you can't. If you believe you are crazy for hearing voices or seeing visions, then you will push them away or fight them, making you crazy. If you allow them, believe in them, and are open to those same visions and voices, then perhaps magic could happen. You get to implant whatever placebo you wish into your mind.

For example, the belief that, "You have limitless potential." You can apply this to any subject. If you believe that, then your brain is going to generate thoughts that make you feel limitless. As your brain is creating more and more thoughts around this belief, your body will start feeling more and more limitless by the emotional empowerment that you are receiving by your thoughts and beliefs. What type of actions and behaviors do you think will follow if you were feeling confident and having consistent thoughts about how limitless you are? You would behave in a way with high energy and in alignment with the placebo placed inside of your mind. You would ask out that girl you have a crush on at work, go for that job promotion or start your own business, or book the plane ticket to that country you always wanted to visit. You would constantly grow and put yourself out of your comfort zone by doing new things because you're not bound by limits. You will eventually break out of the boxes of imprisonment. You become limitless and closer than you would have without that powerful belief.

Let's take this in the other direction to say your belief is, "Your potential has a limit in who you can become and what you can do." If you truly believe this, then your brain will create a ceiling over your potential, and generate thoughts to convince you of this belief. Your brain will create more and more thoughts and look for more and more evidence of why this is true.

Your body will pull back so that you won't hit that ceiling, which causes your emotions to be limited to your goals. Uncertainty would take hold throughout your behaviors and actions, because you may believe you can achieve a lot, or believe nothing can be achieved, so you might as well settle. What do you think your results will be with this belief? Maybe you will lose 10 pounds, but you could never lose 40. You will not ask that guy out. He's out of your league, plus girls shouldn't ask guys out anyway. You will not travel to another country because you've never left your hometown. You will stay in the boxes where you have lived your whole life. Perhaps you may break out of a few, but there's only so many that you can remove until one box is big enough to limit you to your level of belief about your own potential.

Which belief would you prefer? I choose limitless. Perhaps there are limits to our potential, but does it matter? If you act with your beliefs, then you will go much further in life having an outrageous, empowering belief, whether or not it's delusional. Of course, there are other beliefs that surround the concept of being limitless or not, in which you would find clarity.

This same placebo applies to whether God exists. Does it matter? I would rather believe in some high power speaking to me, giving me insight, guiding my path, presenting magic all around me, blessing me, carrying all of my burdens, and giving me superhuman strength to actualize my potential for a meaningful life. Then, when I die, I may find out that it was all make believe, but fuck it. I lived a full and joyous life by taking chances and going for my dreams. The choice is up to you. Does what you believe in empower or disempower you? I encourage you to lean towards empowerment.

As far as my dream goes, whatever I had experienced was exactly what I needed at that moment in time. The dream started with me standing in front of a council of three. Perhaps they were spirit guides or maybe they were angels, but again, that didn't matter. I knew they were higher beings of authority. They told me I had been happy for my entire life. They told me to think back to the moment in which I made that choice to be happy. Instantly, I warped back to when I was three, when I consciously chose to be happy.

I made that choice not for myself, but for my sisters, for my mom, for my family, for them, not me. I didn't want to cause anyone more stress. I didn't want to take attention away from my sisters since I was the youngest. I didn't want to be seen, and I didn't want to be heard. If I was an obedient little boy that did everything he was supposed to, then maybe everyone would be happy, or at least I wouldn't cause their unhappiness. I didn't want to create problems for anyone, so I smiled and acted like everything was okay.

The council brought me back and told me I've spent my life doing this exact thing in every situation, and for every person who I cared about. It served me well. I did it with pure love. I gave my power to all those who needed power. I was happy for them, and that helped them find happiness in themselves. Now, it was time for me to choose to be happy for myself. This would be the only way that I could move forward on my journey. Then, I snapped out of my dream and woke up.

I lay there, overwhelmed by my experience. My whole life replayed in my mind, going over the different areas of my life. Tears were rolling down my cheeks as I'm realizing the truth of the words from this wise council. I didn't just make that decision as a child, but this cycle has been repeated with my family, in sports, with friends, in marriage, in relationships, with my son, with clients, and with everyone and everywhere.

I thought I was giving everything I had to my marriage for years, trying to make sure she was happy and that she felt loved. I was always complaining about how I wasn't being loved in the amount I deserved. The girl that I dated following my split loved me relentlessly, and was teaching me how to love myself. I couldn't come close to reciprocating that love, as my cup was empty. Mackenna gave me her life, but it didn't matter what she did, or didn't do, I couldn't receive it. I wasn't loving myself, and if I can't do that, then how do I expect myself to love someone else, or fully receive love from someone? The answer is, I can't. The quality and quantity of love are in direct correlation to the amount of love I was experiencing within my heart and soul.

I even thought about my relationship with Greyson. I give him all of my power and attention 100% while I'm with him. There are so many days where I feel drained after spending time with him. I thought it was because I was working hard at being a good father, but in reality, I didn't know how to fill up my cup when I was with him.

Finally, I reflected on what I believed my life's purpose to be. I always viewed it as though I was supposed to save people from their unfulfilled lives, as if I was some sort of hero or something. I wanted to help them feel more empowered, happy, and loved so they could actualize their potential. That sounds great, but what I would do in our coaching calls was talk more than my clients would. I would give them the answers to the questions I asked of them. I wasn't coaching. I was giving them my empowerment; my love, my happiness, and they weren't receiving the wanted results.

It was because I didn't help them uncover these things within themselves. I was providing the energy, rather than coaching them in finding the source of where their energy came from, which is in every one of us. We have all heard the saying, "Give a man a fish, and he eats for a day. Teach a man to fish, and he eats for a lifetime." I was giving my clients the fish, rather than teaching them how to fish.

These might seem like different scenarios from the outside, but my core belief was based on an agreement I made with myself when I was three. I carried this core belief around with me, giving me the same results at the end of each experience; I gave everything I could to something for someone and I thought that if I would try harder that I would get a different result; but no matter what I did, I was left feeling drained, burnt out, unloved, unaccepted, unworthy, bitter, and alone. This is the power of our core belief, and I discovered the one that had been blocking me from everything that I wanted in life—Self-love and Acceptance. Now, how do I live in this new space I desire? Little did I know what was coming to me.

CHAPTER 17
UNCOVERING THE INNER HERO

I was excited to get away for the weekend.

I looked at the upcoming workshop as an opportunity to reconnect and further explore the information I received from my dream. The workshop was scheduled for a Saturday, so on Friday, I took the five-hour trip from Vegas to El Matador Beach in Malibu.

I arrived early in the afternoon and spent the day on the beach in the sun. I explored some of the nearby caves and then I jumped into the ocean. I love the cold water of the Pacific Ocean. Before I got into cold water exposure and ice baths, I enjoyed jumping into the ocean. I felt as if it shocked my body to the point of awakening the soul. It would make me feel cleansed, lighter, and energized as if I just took off a thousand pound backpack and left it for the ocean to handle. I couldn't go to the ocean without jumping in, and this time was no different.

Since the pandemic of 2020 hit, I hadn't gone to the ocean. It had been nearly a year, and this was the longest time I had spent away from the Big Blue. I jumped in the water and embraced the cold, softening every muscle, taking deep relaxing breaths, bobbing up and down with the waves while soaking up every bit of that beautiful moment.

After, I dried off to meditate. I don't know about you, but closing your eyes and absorbing the sounds of a beach is enriching. My intention was to sit for 30 minutes while repeating a mantra I liked on Instagram. It was from Brad Harkema, the lead coach of the upcoming workshop. "My body is at ease, and my body feels safe to receive."

I closed my eyes, connected with the silence within and emptied my mind of any distractions. My senses heightened, allowing me to become one with my environment. No thoughts, but directing my focus on repeating the mantra, "My body is at ease, and my body feels safe to receive."

Even though I was 40 yards from the ocean, it felt as if the waves were crashing on top of me with every synchronized exhale. I began eavesdropping on the seagull's conversations. I was smiling towards the sun and receiving the sun's smile back. I laughed as I faintly heard the laughter of a family in the distance, and sank deeper and deeper into the infinite grains of sand shifting between my toes. With each repetition of the mantra, "My body is at ease, and my body feels ready to receive," I felt more and more at peace, except for that one thing creeping in. I was still wet from the five-minute ocean plunge, and my body had not warmed up from the freezing cold water. It was a gorgeous December day, and the sun was glowing. There was a chill in the air. My thoughts wandered to, "Maybe it's time to put a sweater on? It's getting cold. Damnit, now my body is shivering. Nope, just ease into it! You got this. My body is at ease, and my body feels ready to receive. I'll be more comfortable if I just put on my sweater."

It lasted 15 minutes until I caved. I opened my eyes, grabbed my sweater, put it over my head, and as soon as my head popped through the hoody, a pod of dolphins caught my eyes. In the exact moment my thoughts were leading me to put on my sweater, I was being led to a magical moment watching a family of dolphins playing in the ocean. For the next three minutes, I gazed out into the ocean with a heart full of appreciation. They didn't care what was going on in the world, didn't care about making money, or about what kind of difference they were going to make. They were just BEING, flowing with life, living fully. I watched as they playfully engaged with a paddle boarder for a few moments, and then they vanished into the horizon.

A permanent smile glazed across my face for the remaining 10 minutes of my meditation. I got lost inside of myself, feeling connected with the divine. I'd say the remaining time was 10 minutes, but it felt like two. I felt like I was exactly where I was supposed to be at that moment in time, and nothing else mattered. Tears rolled down my face. I felt loved. I felt connected, and I felt whole. Following my meditation, I spent the next 20 minutes journaling about my experience and setting my intentions for the workshop. I wrote my intention as if I had just woken up Monday morning, and I'm reflecting backwards on all the experiences that I received over the weekend. Below is a portion of my entry that I wrote on the beach.

"Good morning, world. Thank you for all of your beauty. I see and I hear you. I am completely in love with you, and every bit of what you offer. This weekend was absolutely amazing, and I received more than I could have ever expected. I found a piece of myself that I had forgotten. I feel completely alive. I found my fire and passion, as it is no longer dormant, and I will not hide it ever again! Everything is always working out for me, and this weekend is yet more proof of that. Everything is ok Jonathon, and it truly works out in perfect timing as that is how the universe functions. I know this because all the experiences before this weekend led me here to find this part of Jonathon that I had forgotten. Now that I remember this part of myself, I am looking forward to living in alignment with this upgraded version of who I am, and let it continue to unfold and expand more than I can even comprehend. I finally got it. I finally feel like me. This must be what it is like to be aligned with my Inner Hero."

After I finished my entry, I closed my journal, took one more deep breath, and said goodbye to the beach. The next morning, I woke up early to do an incredible hike with a close friend that lives in the Los Angeles area. We could connect, laugh, have deep expansive conversations, then have some breakfast. Leaving him, I felt charged and ready for the day ahead. I was off to the Mystic Mansion for the workshop.

With all the COVID-19 restrictions across the world, and especially in California, I wasn't sure about the restrictions at the workshop. I'm not a fan of masks, and I didn't want to have to wear one all day while trying to connect and be vulnerable with a group of strangers. I wanted to see people's smiles, and I wanted to show mine. It's healing to see the bare emotion of the human face.

When I arrived, there were a few individuals standing in the mansion's courtyard. They weren't letting anyone in, as they first wanted to conduct a COVID-19 test before entering. Little did I know that an influencer, Pavel Stuchlik, who led me to the workshop, was also the co-founder of a company called Wellness 4 Humanity. I attended a mini workshop with Pavel before. He and another Wim Hof instructor led us through the Wim Hof Breathing Method followed by sun gazing at Red Rock Canyon in Las Vegas. I was unaware that he was going to be a huge part of this workshop. Stuchlik's NOAIAON Movement was how I knew him. The NOAIAON lifestyle is a 7-component lifestyle of meditation, prayer or divine communion, light diet, treating your body as a temple, selfless service, silence and nature, and singing or listening to sacred music.

Stuchlik's mission is to host festivals, but the intention is that when taking part in his events that people don't need a week to recover because of the drugs, but it is an event to be recharged. He is an incredible leader and his story is epic. After COVID-19 hit, he put his mission on hold. He shifted gears by co-creating a conscious way to test for COVID-19 so that people could meet in person in a safe environment. These tests allowed you to get an accurate COVID-19 reading within 15 to 20 minutes. By using these test kits, we could be interactive at a 12-hour workshop.

As I was waiting for my test to come back, I was feeling uncomfortable. My anxiety was rising, and my mind was racing. "What am I doing here? I know nothing about this workshop, other than its title, Humans I Trust, which doesn't automatically mean I should trust them, and that it's supposed to host spiritual entrepreneurs."

I'm an open person and I rarely go into experiences with expectations. I set my intention and then let go by allowing the process to unfold in whatever way it naturally does. This experience was no different, but spirituality is a very broad topic. This could be a group of nudists here for an orgy to express their spiritual freedom. Perhaps this was a plant medicine workshop, and I was going to partake in psilocybin or ayahuasca? I did not know what I was about to walk into, and I didn't give it a second thought until that moment. I just said, "Fuck it, I'm already here. I was led here for a reason and I'll be open to whatever happens. If it's too much for me, I always have the option to leave, but I came here to get out of my comfort zone. Just embrace it. Everything will be alright. Everything is always working out for me. My body is at ease, and my body feels safe to receive."

My test came back clear, and I sparked up conversations with the other participants. My anxiety dwindled. In the background, I could hear a woman singing beautiful Sanskrit. She was clearing the inside of the mansion with prayer, sage, and song. It felt majestic and magical. She walked out of the mansion to greet us. Before we could enter, she was going to say a prayer over us, while saging our energy. Directly behind her, another person walked out of the mansion.

I laughed to myself, thinking, "What the fuck did I just get myself into?" After seeing this man, I definitely thought he was tripping on some great LSD or Ecstasy.

This guy was grinning so hard that he could barely keep his eyes open. I had never seen someone so happy. He was dressed in light flowing clothes, his neck and wrists covered with an assortment of crystals, and he wore a bright purple and sparkly baseball cap with a single giant eye on the front, and a shawl wrapped across his shoulders down to his hands that he was flapping as if it were his wings. He had this contagious high-pitched giggle that came from the depths of his soul. It was pure joy at its finest, and that scared the shit out of me.

This guy's name was Dragon. Dragon Love. He was comfortable in his own skin, and that was making me uncomfortable in mine. I wanted to run to the nearest corner and shrink into a tiny ball. I didn't realize it at that moment, but he was someone I needed to meet during this workshop. He was the lead in the inner child exercise later that day.

Destiny Dharma was the beautiful voice that was radiating throughout the mansion and the courtyard. She was a coach and a channeler for the workshop. It was my turn to be saged and to be prayed over. I closed my eyes, opened my arms out wide and received the blessings showered upon me. While Destiny was singing, Dragon was sprinkling flower petals over me. When I opened my eyes, Destiny, Brad, and Dragon greeted me with a hug.

Dragon held me longer than the other two. He embraced me for at least 30 seconds. The longer he held on to me, the more I felt my body soften by releasing all its tension. His heart was penetrating me with pure love. After we split apart, he gazed straight into my eyes, as I gazed into his for another 30 seconds. We smiled into each other; tears flowed down both of our cheeks. No longer did I feel uncomfortable with this human, rather, I felt as if I was home. Dragon was an ordinary man that embodied the energy of the loving Christ.

Many spiritual teachers will tell you that as you witness the gifts that other spiritual coaches and teachers possess, you may think to yourself, "Wow, they have something special. They have supernatural abilities." The thing is, we are ALL capable of these supernatural gifts and abilities. We were born with them. We must learn how to tune into them by paying attention and develop them by enhancing our awareness of them.

One of the first individuals that I met in this workshop was an energy reader and an intuitive artist named Chantel. I asked her to do a reading on me and to draw on a mirror what she saw and felt within my energy field. We both got into a meditative state, and she spoke out what she was interpreting while reading my energy, while also drawing symbols on the mirror. She was speaking about all the things I had experienced in the last week. The first thing she told me was that my inner child wanted to tell me something. He wanted to give me permission to play. He told her it was safe to play, and that this was my destiny when I came here to earth. It was safe for me to let go, to be free.

A vision came to me. I was the three-year-old self that I had witnessed just a week prior in my dream, and I was running around in a meadow full of brightly colored wildflowers. Giant trees surrounded the edges of the meadow; I wasn't alone though, Greyson was with me. He was my friend, and we were playing and laughing together. I was so happy watching Greyson play. He was so good at it, so free. He paused and looked at me through a smile, and told me that the only reason he knows how to play with such a free spirit is because his father taught him how; that I taught him how. I taught him through the way I lived my life, and now it's time for him to teach me so that his father can teach him.

I have always had this energetic intuition that Greyson is some sort of guide, or a wise shaman. I believe that his dharma, or life mission, is to help others step into their true divine power. This has been true for my life from the moment he was in the womb, to the first few months after he was born, and now, to this moment in time during this spiritual vision. He was the spirit of a wise and old soul.

As we were finishing up our session, I continued to reflect on my vision and my interpretation. It is said that time is not linear, which I don't fully understand, but I believe that parts of ourselves and others can come in and out of different dimensions of time to give and receive messages. There is a part at the end of the movie, *Harry Potter and The Prisoner of Azkaban*, that Harry was getting his soul sucked out, near a pond, by hundreds of these dark entities that fed off of human happiness, known as Dementors. Across from the pond he saw a light that was in the shape of a white stag, which he believed to be his dead father, coming to rescue him with a magical Patronus spell. This powerful magic is to warn off these dark creatures, and it did just that.

Later in the movie, Harry gets ahold of a timepiece that his friend Hermione had. They both went back in time to fix a few occurrences that had happened in the past day.

The time traveling Harry found himself across the pond, watching in the distance the day before, as if watching a replay of his life, as these Dementors were sucking out his soul. Time traveling Harry told Hermione to watch and wait as he believed his father was going to come and save him. His father never came, and with that realization, he cast his Patronus spell to send off all the Dementors to save himself across the pond. The magic was far beyond his capabilities. Hermione asked how he knew he could do that, and he said, "Because I've already done it before." In reality, that was his first time casting a spell of that magnitude, but he witnessed himself doing it before that moment, which gave him faith that he could do it again.

This is what I believe the energy of time is like. Maybe you won't physically see yourself experience a time warp, but you may have a powerful experience through visualization. It happens all the time to myself and other spiritual leaders that I know. If this is true, then who knows that ripple effect in time and space and how it affects our lives and experiences. You may receive deep healing by going backwards into the past to support yourself through a traumatic experience, or move forward in time to meet with your future self for wisdom and answers to difficult situations in the present moment.

I believe a part of Greyson came to me in this vision as an image that I could recognize, so that he could give me permission to be myself and play. He gave me the insight that my future self had figured out, and that's why he was how he was. If I taught him, then that means I should know how to do it. How do I move forward with that truth with faith? Just like Harry did, "Because I've already done it before."

Chantel continued the energy work with me, and walked me through each part of her intuitive mirror drawing. It was insightful and was definitely the perfect way to prepare me for the rest of the day. Although I missed out on the first group exercise, I knew I was where I was supposed to be in that moment, one-on-one with this gifted energy healer.

Following my experience with Chantel, I went to meet the rest of the group outside in the backyard to join in a circle. We were going into the inner child work of the day. I was nervous to take part in this exercise. I had done some healing with my inner child moments before with Chantel, so I felt resistance to go deeper in front of everyone else. This is when I also found out that Dragon was leading this experience. He was extremely bouncy and giggly. Every time he looked your way, it seemed as if he was gazing into you, rather than at you. He saw who you really were, rather than what you thought you were. He could see past the surface of my mask.

He started the session by explaining the innate freedom of the inner child. When we were children, we cried when we wanted to, laughed when we wanted to, and played when we wanted to. We did whatever inspired us with no worries about how others would perceive or judge us.

At some point, we were programmed to withhold our innate desires. We would start trying to fit in more, instead of allowing ourselves to stand out as our unique selves. This is where the masks are born. We would inherit masks from people around us based on their own insecurities and judgements. Usually, our parents and siblings were the first ones to project these masks onto us.

As we move on in life, the programming gets deeper and deeper and we drift away from our inner child, and we drift away from our innate freedom of the uniqueness of our soul. Dragon told us that our birthrights fade. Children become quiet, they don't want to be seen, and they feel unloved; but in reality our true birthrights are,

"We are meant to be seen. We are meant to be heard. We are meant to be loved."

This made complete and logical sense to me, as this is what I knew to be true in my life; while also getting to see what that freedom looks like through the eyes and energy of how Greyson lived his day-to-day life since the day he was born. When he was hungry, he cried. When he wanted to be held, he cried. When he was uncomfortable, he cried. Something he didn't like, or he wanted, he cried. Tired, he slept. Happy, he smiled or laughed. When we were in a restaurant and something exciting happened, he would scream with joy, not caring who heard him. At the playground, he is silly and likes to dance around without the concern of others watching him or judging him. Greyson was free to be Greyson without restriction. He's upset one moment, while completely okay and happy the next. He didn't attach to the past. However he felt in the present moment, he would feel and embody every aspect of that emotion. There is no past, or future—only right now.

Dragon continued the session by having us laugh out loud as hard as we could, no matter how uncomfortable it may feel. At first everyone was laughing softly and you could tell that we were all forcing it, except for Dragon. Dragon was cracking up with an intense belly laugh. I noticed that the more I was laughing and watching others laugh, my laugh became genuine. I laughed so hard that I was in tears. My abs were hurting, and my cheeks were aching because of my big smile. After two minutes of laughing, we settled down. He explained we could shift the state of our consciousness by simply laughing. Our brain releases chemicals that flood the body, which change our whole physiological structure.

Now that something had shifted our physiology, it was time for us to be present in our body by tuning inward and acting out how it feels to be silly again. Dragon instructed us to close our eyes, tune out the other people, and act as if we were in our inner child's body. He encouraged us to dance, to jump up and down, to play, and to laugh. For another few minutes, we moved in whatever ways our bodies inspired us to move. Eventually, he had us open our eyes and dance with each other. I was still a little uncomfortable taking part in this exercise, but I felt lighter in my body, and I was definitely having fun playfully dancing around with everyone else.

The next part of the session was to now BE your younger self before the program, as the inner child, rather than to ACT like your inner child. So we were directed to think about the version of ourselves in which we didn't care who was watching, and just do what inspired us as if we were our younger selves. They encouraged us to talk like kids or babies, play games together, and be as silly as we wanted. He encouraged us to remember this part of ourselves and just BE whatever that meant for each one of us. Before we started, Dragon, Destiny, and Brad walked around to each of us, looked us straight in the eyes, and reminded us of our birthright. "You are meant to be seen. You are meant to be heard. You are meant to be loved."

I felt myself shut down when I tried to remember who I was. I couldn't remember a time where I felt free to be me. Earlier this week, I had discovered that I made a choice to be obedient and a good little boy at three. I had always been someone who waited for permission to play or be wild. I couldn't remember a time before trauma, as I had lived with trauma from almost the time of my birth. My first instinct was to go run to the corner and sit against the wall to watch the other kids play as I remember doing as long as I could recall. I didn't want to be seen. I didn't want to be loud. I would rather not create any attention towards myself. I felt like I couldn't let go of my control, since I had been in control of my actions from as far back as I could remember. I didn't want to let my inner child come out. I wanted to hide. I didn't feel that they would love me if I were authentically me. I didn't feel like they would accept me as the true Jonathon.

Right before I headed towards the corner of the backyard, Brad came up and talked to me with a lisp, as if he was a small child. He asked if I wanted to play with him. I embodied my insecure little self. I looked down at the ground to avoid eye contact, and in a very shy, and soft toned whisper I murmured, "Yes, I would really like that." He then asked me what I wanted to play, and without hesitation I looked up at him while blurting out, "Tag! Do you wanna play tag? I really like tag." "Okay." Receiving my suggestion, Brad then tapped my shoulder. "You're it!" From there, that dark shadow that had this overwhelming weight of insecurity of not being enough and not being included, vanished.

It took an invitation to be myself, by someone else being themself. We ran around tagging others, screaming, "You're it!" Soon we had a group of ten playing hide and seek. We were all laughing so hard while playing this game that we all played as children. I had so much fun being free, being silly, and being me. After five minutes, I paused in immense gratitude and decided that I wanted to lie down on the grass so I could look up at the sky. I spent the next few minutes with a smile across my face that radiated from my soul, staring off into the clouds as they drifted by. I was present within myself, identifying each traveling cloud with the animal shape.

In that moment, my inner child spoke to the adult me and whispered, "Thank you, Jonathon, for allowing yourself to play with me. You are meant to be seen. You are meant to be heard. You are meant to be loved. There are many people who want to see you, who would like to hear what you have to say, and who would love to love you. Just be you, and everything else will fall into place."

During this session, I could team up with my inner child and reshape how I would have wanted to be as a child, even if it wasn't the way I actually was as my little self. I finally had the permission that I needed to be me, by having an invitation to be me, no one else, just Jonathon. That's who I came here to be, and in this moment, I understood what that meant. I have used the mantra that I learned that day repeatedly since then. "I am meant to be seen. I am meant to be heard. I am meant to be loved." Not only have I seen a dramatic energy shift within, but also in the way I have been parenting Greyson, as he is meant to be seen, meant to be heard, and meant to be loved as he is.

After the inner child exercise, we came inside to join in a cacao ceremony. Cacao is the pure form of chocolate, which helps open up the heart center. We went around in the circle to introduce ourselves and express our intentions for the workshop. This is where I learned that Dragon Love was not as hippie dippie as I first thought. He has a PhD in Counseling Psychology and studied Theology. He created the Give Shirt, in hopes of raising consciousness about the power of giving. This is not just about helping others, but also how giving allows the giver to receive more happiness in life. All proceeds go to a variety of charities. If you would like to support him and his mission go to thegiveshirt.com

When it was my turn, I expressed that my intention was to remember a piece of myself that I had forgotten along my journey. I told them about some of the work I did with Chantel and how I had already received so much out of this workshop in the first few hours. I shared with them the dream I had earlier in the week and how it applied to the inner child work we had just completed. Following the ceremony, we went into the breath work led by Pavel. This by far was why I came here to the Mystic Mansion.

•

Pavel is what I would consider a modern day shaman. He is 30-years-old, was a professional cyclist, successful entrepreneur, a father, and a leader. A diagnosis of an autoimmune disease ended his cycling career before it could really take off. This propelled him on a spiritual journey to learn how to heal his body. He went to different retreats around the world, eating healthy, taking part in plant medicine, cold water exposure, breath work, ecstatic dance, music, and eventually spending ten days in a cave in Thailand fasting with only water. Imagine spending ten days in a dark cave, with yourself, with only water? He told us that is where he lost his mind to find himself. In that cave, he came up with the name NOAIAON. Later learning, NOA means movement; AON is all or none. With #noamovment NOAIAON is bringing people back to their center of union with others. His story is one of the most powerful stories I have ever heard, and this quick introduction does not do him justice. Certified in the Wim Hof Method, he spends every day practicing it for himself. Ever since he discovered Wim's method, he has never been sick.

The Wim Hof Breathing Method, meditation, healing beats and sound are all part of the unique NOAIAON experience created by Pavel. All 22 of us lay down in a circle on our yoga mats, with our heads pointed towards the middle of the room. The lights dimmed. We wore blindfolds and headphones so we couldn't hear or see anyone. We immersed ourselves in our experience with no external distractions.

Pavel briefly explained what we were getting ready to experience. We were going to do seven rounds of intense intentional breathing. Pavel was taking us on an internal journey to connect deeper with ourselves to heal the past, receive messages from our higher self and subconscious, along with experiencing a neurological system reset. The specifics about HOW I got to this internal journey aren't as important as WHAT I received from this experience and what happened on the other side. When you go into a deep state of consciousness like this, where you get voices and visions as I have received time and time again, you tap into a whole other realm or dimensional reality. The experience of this realm is as real as if you and I sat down for a coffee at a busy Starbucks to have a deep and expansive conversation about the constructs of life. We would both leave feeling empowered, gaining insights, and perhaps knowing each other on a more intimate level. It would be an experience with a memory attached.

This realm, or dimensional reality, is a world within your consciousness, and your consciousness would like to show you and tell you who and what it is, by uncovering who and what YOU are. It is the process of consciousness experiencing consciousness through an intimate embodied interaction. You will perceive it as a REAL experience in which you feel empowered; you will gain insights, and perhaps know yourself and your consciousness on a more intimate level.

Just because it's not happening externally does not mean it's not real, and that it happened. Everything that you experience is actually being experienced in your head. Your mind is the interpreter of the world around you. Your brain is encapsulated in complete darkness within a skull; yet it sees light, hears, tastes, feels, smells, and experiences emotion through the brain's translation of different vibrational interpretations. So what is real? Is anything real? Or is real subjective, based on each individual's interpretation of their experiences, whether it's external or internal? You can't see thoughts or emotions, yet they exist and most people would say they are real.

I wanted to go deep into what reality is and to set the foundation on the experience I received during this breath work. This doesn't mean if you do this breath work, you will experience what I experienced. Your reality will look completely different; while having a personalized and intimate interaction with your consciousness based on your past, where you are today, and the desires you have for your future. So meditation is such a powerful tool, as this is where you uncover deeper knowledge, healing, and awareness of self.

At the workshop, Pavel led us to a slow start by helping us synchronize our breathing with one another. He helped us get into a flow by following his voice, and by the music he intentionally chose. The sounds and music were all at a specific frequency, 528 hertz. The known frequency is its connection to the vibrations and frequency found in the natural world. We also consider it to be the frequency of love; that restores human consciousness and brings more harmony and balance into your life. It can help create self-love and can end the problems of illness, hatred, and jealousy in the world.

We did about seven rounds of this intense breathing method. After the first round of breathing, my body was vibrating. Literally, every cell in my body felt tingly. The deeper we went, the more my body was vibrating, until there was a point where I didn't have a body. I was no-body. I lost touch with where I was, who was around me, and melted into my mind's consciousness. Pavel was still guiding me, but his voice was more like background noise. I was in a deep, hypnotic state of consciousness. If I was connected to a machine that measured my brain waves, I was going in and out of theta, and gamma. I would compare this state of euphoria to having an intense psychedelic experience, yet, no psychedelics were involved—only sounds and breath. This type of breath work is not new. It's been around for thousands of years and has had different names. We have reintroduced breath work to our world through eastern influence and modern day influencers.

The Iceman, Wim Hof, is not the only one promoting this magical breathing technique, as Dr. Joe Dispenza has also been promoting the healing and spiritual benefits of similar meditations and breath work. In eastern culture, they might call this Kundalini. Scientifically, what is happening is that by doing this intense breathing repeatedly, while squeezing or flexing the lower end of your body to the top of your head, you are pushing your cerebral fluid into your brainstem, through the vagus nerve, and up into your pineal gland also known as the Third Eye Energy Center or Chakra.

By tapping into this center of the brain, you're not only allowing healing effects to take place for your body, you can also experience a total and natural DMT release, causing you to have a natural psychedelic experience. This means, by having a natural psychedelic experience, you are having a real biological and psychological experience, or you may have visions or hear voices that seem to be real inside of your mind. Sounds scary, but it's actually a loving experience that feels like ecstasy.

At this point in this session, I am completely euphoric and I am immersed within this vivid internal dream world. As we were laying there, Pavel instructed us to go back in time to greet our inner child. He said that our inner child had something for us, something that we had forgotten, and it was time to remember. We were ready to remember.

My heart instantly expanded, as I knew why I was there at that workshop. I was in the perfect place at the perfect time. I was in direct alignment with the intention that I had set for myself for the weekend. As my heart opened up, I shot back in time to when I was three years old, to the moment before I made that decision to be happy for everyone else around me. I saw my inner child, not having a physical body, but I was a white and golden body of light. Visualizing this version of myself was overwhelmingly beautiful. I was absolutely perfect. This little boy I was observing was so strong, so powerful, and so loving. He was pure.

I continued to watch him, and understand on a deeper level what my dream meant from the week before. From this space of perfection and power, I gave away my light to those around me, gave away my strength to those who needed strength. I lent out my power to those that felt powerless, and sent loving light to the ones who lacked love. I had been doing this my whole life. I was giving away this eternal power to others while not harnessing it to charge my being. My cup was empty. In that moment of understanding, I was told by an eminent authority that I may not give this power away any longer. I was told that this light body was meant for the vessel of Jonathon, and I should honor it as a gift. The more that I harness this loving light by embodying it, and aligning with it in my daily life, the more it will show others how to harness it for themselves. Each of us has an eternal flame inside. I must teach others how to honor the light inside, rather than to give them mine. Jonathon's light body was meant for Jonathon, and not for the surrounding people.

From that point, Pavel prompted us to unzip our "body suits." He told us to imagine that there was a zipper from our belly button to the top of our head and down the back of our spine. It was time to unzip ourselves out of our skin, the vessel where our souls live. I visualized taking the zipper and zipping out of my body suit. As soon as I did, my spirit expanded out of my body and my childhood best friend Michael, greeted me.

I was sobbing nearly the entire time, as well as laughing, smiling, shaking, and even experiencing immense anger. The energy stored in the cells of my brain and body from the trauma experienced in my lifetime was being released, and I felt every bit of it. It felt as if I was shedding a thousand pound weight that I had been carrying around with me for most of my life.

•

When Michael greeted me, he had an enormous smile on his face. He was so delighted to see me, as I was to see him. He reached out his hand, pulled me out of my vessel, leaving my body suit on the ground, and then embraced me. I was crying pretty hard, mostly out of joy, but I was also crying because I had missed my best friend so much in the past five years.

Here he was, standing right in front of me, hugging me and holding me. I felt so much gratitude for him in that moment, as he was the reason I chose the path that I was on, and from his influence why I was transforming my life. I wanted to share this with him, and everything else that had happened since he had left; yet he already knew how I felt. He told me to save my words. He was here to speak to me, not the other way around.

We started walking side by side. He told me that everything was okay, and that he was okay. He continued to explain to me that what I perceive in the physical realm differs from how it is being experienced in the non-physical realm. I saw him as someone who died, but in all truth, he stated he was alive, more alive than he has ever been. He's not living as he once was, but he was living within Jonathon's vessel. Not only was he completely alive in my vessel, but also he was living through the physical vessels of each one of his family members and friends. The more we allow him to exist within our experiences without resisting his aliveness, the more he exists. Perceived death is to die, while perceived life is to live.

He expanded on this concept by telling me he didn't just exist in the ones who knew him, but in all physical beings. Michael said that we had nothing to fear in death, as death is just an illusion. Death is the transition into a new beginning. All of existence was an illusion. All suffering was an illusion, which was created by our doing. He told me it didn't stop with him experiencing life through our vessels, but I too, was experiencing life through the surrounding vessels. Each person around me is a mirror and can be shared to know my true self better.

We all share the same source, the same oneness, and the only separation is the vessel itself. The spirit is of the same origin. Michael reminded me of the powerful and eternal light I had witnessed while observing my inner child; and explained that when my body suit gets old and shriveled, then goes to sleep, that same powerful light being released from the vessel is the same constant source of energy it had been when entering the physical plain. It is the Alpha and the Omega, an unchangeable, all powerful, all knowing energy that is within each of us from the moment we enter our physical bodies, to the moment we leave. It is the beginning and the end, yet there is no beginning, and there is no end, but it is eternally transitioning. When the physical body dies, the light body, or soul part of us, is greeted back to the oneness of All That Is. It is not gone, but it changes form, and we then experience existence through the ones who carried our vibrational frequency in their field. It transmuted us into the experience of being alive, in the surrounding vessels, without the physical block of our vessel. We are free to just BE, with no separation, suffering or pain, through a full oneness with the Source of all Creation.

Michael ended our conversation by reinforcing that he still exists and that I will still exist far beyond this physical life; and that our impact is an everlasting ripple effect across all time, space, dimension, and reality. We are eternal, and each of us a part of the whole, which means we are in all actuality, the Whole. We each came here to play a specific role, and it's important for me to play my role full out. I was instructed to no longer give my power away, but teach others how to harness their eternal power, by the way I harness it for myself through example. This is what it is to embody self-love and to actualize potential. Everything else is just a self-created illusion that is manifested by the separation of our true nature. The more separated we are from our true self, the more suffering we will experience.

He embraced me with a hug one more time, telling me, "I love you. You are doing a great job. You are ALL doing a great job." I believe he was referring to all of us as humanity, but I think he was addressing his family and friends. After those last words, we synergized into one spirit. My spirit expanded, and I felt an overwhelming comfort wash over me.

•

Pavel instructed us to pick up our body suits from the ground and wash them, as if it were our favorite outfit. At first, when I picked up my body suit, it felt dirty. It felt tainted and abused. I washed and then I massaged it, then loved it, apologized to it, and gave thanks to it for serving me the way it had for the last 30 years. I had an overwhelming feeling that as much gratitude that I had for my vessel in that moment, I no longer felt it belonged to me. It felt as if I had outgrown it, and if I tried to put it back on, it wouldn't fit. Suddenly a fire presented itself to me, so I said my goodbyes to my bodysuit as I felt an urge to throw it into the fire. The fire burned my vessel to ashes, completely disintegrating it into tiny particles. From there, a bright white light formed over the fire and acted as a magnet, attracting and pulling each of those particles upward into the white light. The particles were being sucked up out of the fire like a vacuum to form and recreate a new body suit for me. A large vessel of light was manifesting before me, made of golden armor. I could hardly look directly at this new body suit as it beamed like the sun. I was told that this was my new vessel, as it will hold the light that was meant for me to embody in this physical realm.

I have always heard the saying, "My whole life flashed before my eyes," but I never understood how that was possible. That's what happened to me as soon as I put on this upgraded body suit. My whole life flashed before my eyes. It was ALL so clear. My life made sense, as I recognized one of the core paradigms that I had been living my entire life. This agreement that I made with myself as a child was an underlying constant energy that was behind every experience. With this new understanding, I saw every moment, every bit of my suffering, and every decision that I had ever made. I entangled every situation and area of my life with this single belief.

I had learned in the last few years that your belief systems create your reality and your results. What happens when you THINK you believe one way, but life shows you something different? What happens when you create these core beliefs without your awareness? After all, we are not aware of the beliefs that we are not aware of. By seeing how my life had unfolded, I realized that our core beliefs held a strong vibrational foundation for our physical existence. This constant underlying vibrational set point is at a specific vibrational frequency, sending out and receiving signals from the universe. You experience life, and life experiences you through a certain level of consciousness. That level of consciousness is determined by the quality of each of our vibrational set points coming from the core of your being—we created everything in life through OUR core signal. This signal is sending out vibrations, and then life brings you vibrations that MATCH the core signal. We then translate those vibrations by how we interpret the experiences that show up in our life on the physical plane by our level of consciousness. So, depending on the quality of the vibrational set point of your paradigms will depend on the quality of experiences you receive. This cycle will repeat itself until you can elevate your consciousness to a level that replaces your core belief, which will change your vibrational set point, which will change the results that are being experienced in your life. If nothing changes, then we will create experiences that may look different but are ultimately giving us the same emotional results. Therefore, the suffering we experience in our lifetime is a self-induced illusion based on our core beliefs.

To bring this back around to what I had witnessed in this matter of moments, I saw my life through the lenses of these few interconnected and jumbled belief systems.

I don't deserve to be heard. I don't deserve to be seen, and I don't deserve to be loved, but I wanted to be heard, I wanted to be seen, and I wanted to be loved. I have desired this my entire life more than anything; and so I did everything I could to get this through doing things for others, while seeking love, approval, recognition, and acceptance from them in return. I could never receive this from them no matter how much I thought I wanted it, because I didn't FEEL like I deserved it on a vibrational level. This is a huge contradiction in my vibrational foundation.

This is why I have been successful in my life, while feeling empty, unsafe, unloved, and alone. I never felt deserving of this on a core level even if I THOUGHT that's what I wanted or THOUGHT that I believed it. My reality was trying to show me this belief my whole life through the experiences that were being attracted to my reality. I was seeking externally for these validations, giving everything I could to everyone else so I would be loved and accepted, while I never gave it to myself. Everything that I wanted in life would never come to me from the external. No one or nothing was going to save me. There are no heroes. Everything that I was looking to receive from others already existed inside of me. I only had to give myself the permission to be heard, the permission to be seen, and the permission to be loved. I had to be the one who saved me from my self-sabotaging core belief of being unworthy, undeserving and not good enough. It did not matter how much the surrounding people loved me, acknowledged me, accepted me, and approved of me because I never could be that for myself.

Life created an abundance of experiences that matched the exact signals I was sending out. None of these life experiences were real. They were all an illusion constructed by my mind to show me what I was sending out. Perhaps every external situation looked a little different, but they all started with the same intention and ended with the same results. I say this all the time, "How you do anything, is how you do everything." The universe answers all of us in this way. So what did this revelation mean? Everything was an illusion. Life was getting worse for me, yet I was trying harder. The contradiction of my beliefs was separating myself farther apart from my true self, which in return created more suffering.

Finally, after five years of a deep desire to become my future ideal self with contradicting beliefs of unworthiness, I had created such separation and had stretched so far apart, that these beliefs snapped back into each other like a rubber band. I had to surrender everything that I had been attempting to do for others, and honor myself and my suffering. Another way of saying that is, I had to let the old version of myself who functioned with this belief system die. I died when I threw my outdated vessel into the fire in order to receive a new life, to be born again.

Observing the life I had lived, I didn't have any pain, no hard feelings, or no regrets. I didn't feel sadness or anger. Instead, I felt an abundant amount of self-compassion for the life I had lived. I could see that I was trying my absolute best in every area of my life just so someone could love me, while all along I was never alone and I was never alone and was always loved. There was always a bigger part of myself guiding me, directing me, and loving me, but I just couldn't see it until this moment.

The past doesn't exist. It is an illusion. The moment has passed, and all that exists is the present moment. So everything I had ever experienced was an illusion, because none of it existed. The only thing that exists from the past is what I am holding in the moment of right now. Each experience was created by me to remember who I Am. Each illusion was trying to speak to me in order to bring me closer to the alignment of what I Am. I now saw each event in my life as a gift. I now felt completely connected to that eternal light when I witnessed my inner child. I had reconnected, reemerged, remembered, and uncovered what that part of myself truly is—my Inner Hero, God, source energy, The Creator of All That Is, my higher-self, Christ, perfection, love, acceptance, the alpha and omega. It is I. Everything that I had been seeking was there all along. I found it, and it was inside of me since the beginning. I am the Hero that was here to save me. It is the Inner Hero, and now I finally see the perfection of life. Every single moment that happened before that moment brought me to this understanding in perfect timing. I felt whole. The Inner Hero inside of me was all that I needed. By honoring that, it means I am honoring others. By becoming one with my true and highest self allows me to become one with our true and higher selves.

This was a huge Moment of AHA! Yet Pavel wasn't done guiding us, as we had a little further to go on this internal journey. He led us up a flight of stairs. These stairs were all white, and at the top of the stairs was a door outlined with a golden light. The closer I moved towards the door, the more warmth I felt from the other side. I could feel pure love radiating from the other side. It was a familiar feeling, a feeling as if I had arrived. I felt like I was getting ready to be reunited with my home.

I put my hand on the doorknob, slowly turned it, and walked through. As I did, my Inner Hero instructed me to close the door behind me. I felt an immense weight of hesitation come over me. There was one more part I had to let go before I could fully enter this enchanted and holy space. I looked back through the door, down the stairs, and what I saw was my family, my friends, and all the people in the world. I couldn't bring them with me. I had to shut the door on them. I felt myself mourn them and I asked my Inner Hero why can't they come with me? The answer I received was the answer that it had given me for the last week, "This is ALL of their home, but you cannot help them get home unless you know how to get home yourself. You cannot do the work for them. You cannot carry them up the stairs. You cannot open the door for them. You cannot save them, Jonathon. You were never meant to save them. You cannot lead them in if you are locked outside. Your job is to make sure that you enter your home and embody your home every day. You can teach them the processes you learned in your journey by looking within, and they will learn not by your words, but by how you live. It's okay to shut the door, Jonathon. The door may shut, but it stays unlocked. You are not leaving them behind, but you are showing them the way by being courageous enough to go where I Am. As you go through your own self-induced suffering, and discover the illusion of your reality, they too, need to discover the illusions they have been creating in their own lives. When they are ready to surrender, and remember who they are, then I will be there. They need examples of this in order for them to uncover their Inner Hero, for when they knock, I will answer. You cannot knock for them—you cannot save them. You are here because you knocked. Now that I have answered, will you enter?"

With complete trust I shut the door, and promised that I will help others look inside themselves for them to uncover their home, for them to listen to their Inner Hero.

When I turned around, I felt paralyzed with bliss. Angels were all around, cheering me on as if I had finally arrived. They were welcoming me home. I had just entered paradise. This was Eden, this was how heaven was described in the ancient scriptures. Enlightened beings surrounded me, playing music that had never penetrated my ear, and I had witnessed colors I can't even describe with words. I had entered a state of Nirvana. I was one with all that is, all that was, and all that will ever be.

After a few minutes in this space, we returned to our physical bodies. We had been doing this breath work for one hour and fifteen minutes, yet time did not exist during the experience. I woke up into a different world, a different reality. I reflected on the last part of my journey, where I had to shut the door behind me as I entered that state of heaven. If everything I had ever experienced in my life was an illusion, these illusions led me to a place of remembrance. This is the work of each of us. If I am a part of consciousness, and I am the whole of consciousness, then that means the world represents a part and the whole of consciousness as well. When I experienced suffering in my life, I was living out the illusion that was manifested from the separation of my Inner Hero. The world was going through a monumental shift of consciousness, as we were all experiencing suffering during this global pandemic. The collective created this illusion for us to remember who we are, but each part of the collective must do their internal work for the mass collective to benefit.

I had to do the work. I had to save myself. I had to love myself, and I had to accept myself and every part of my life, for me to uncover the home that existed within.

We are on the brink of becoming a collectively enlightened society, but each of us must do our part by remembering who we are.

•

Let me ask you? What has the suffering in your life been trying to communicate to you? What is the belief about yourself behind your suffering? What is the paradigm behind the illusions that keep showing up in your life? How do you self-sabotage? Have you been listening to the Inner Hero, or have you been allowing the Inner Villain to influence you?

The Inner Villain tells you are not good enough. It says that you should feel bad if you are happy when the others surrounding you are suffering. It says you can't do it; you will never change. You are alone; no one cares. No one understands. You are not smart enough. You are undeserving of love. No one wants to hear what you have to say. You are poor, and you can't ever make a difference. You are unworthy!

The truth is you are perfect right now, at this moment. Nothing can change that. You are enough. You are loved and not alone. People want to hear what you have to say. You do make a difference. You are born to be happy. You are here to change the world by how you change your world from within. Do you see it when you look into the mirror? Are you able to accept this truth for yourself, or do your beliefs hold you back from believing this? You get to decide.

So what do you think of my story? Do you think I'm crazy? What is crazy? Living in a world of suffering, self-hate, judgement, shame, guilt, anxiety, depression, and fear is crazy to me. What if you could be crazy enough to believe that you could live in a world where you felt happy, joyful, empowered, loving, and whole; and you actualized your true potential? I believe that that world exists. I am living in that world right now. You can't help anyone out of a place of suffering, if you are suffering. You can't help heal the sick if you are not healthy. You cannot teach the poor how to gain wealth if you are poor. You cannot save the world if you have not saved yourself.

Take ownership of your life and watch your reality transform. I believe in you more than you could ever know. If I can do it, anyone can.

CHAPTER 18
ALIGNED WITH THE INNER HERO

I'm sure you are curious. What happens after you uncover the Inner Hero, and you align with that part of yourself?

Let me start with the term enlightenment. What is enlightenment? The spiritual community uses this word to a point of saturation, without embodying its fullness. Most people see enlightenment as the destination to our spiritual journey, and then, when you experience it, you own it. You become enlightened from that moment forward. Enlightenment is not an award—you don't have it forever. Enlightenment is a state of consciousness that can only be experienced in the present moment. It is a choice and an alignment that is embodied in the present. Enlightened beings go in and out of being enlightened every day. To be enlightened is to choose alignment with your higher self or Inner Hero in every moment.

Why I bring this up is because I had this profound, enlightened experience at this workshop where I uncovered and emerged with my Inner Hero. I experienced so much healing, and my life has been completely different since that day. Yet, my old program tries to interject in my life weekly, and sometimes even daily. I consciously must remember what I learned about myself in that workshop. I consciously have to choose to love myself, and have to decide to fill up my cup before anyone else's. When I fall back into my old program, it's when I'm not being conscious. I lose the state of enlightenment until I come back to my Inner Hero.

I'm happy to say to you, though, I have aligned with my Inner Hero more than I have ever chosen to live in this space before. I would like to share with you what has happened since I have done the Humans I Trust Workshop.

I'll begin with what happened right after the breath work with Pavel. We all gathered around and each person shared what they had undergone. Everyone had a profound shift and internal experience. When it was my turn, as I was one of the last ones to share, I went into detail about all the revelations I received. When I finished, the guy next to me was in awe. He asked me if I was going to write a book and continued to compliment how eloquently I spoke. He said if I wasn't writing a book, then I should consider it, because I have a story people need to hear.

This wasn't the first time that I was told this. In the last five years, people have encouraged me to write a book. I knew I would write one, one day, but it was going to be "one day." It was always the future Jonathon who was going to write it. In my mind I felt it was going to be a lot of work, and I had to spend hours upon hours typing it out, or writing it by hand, so when people asked if I was going to write a book, I always answered with, "One day."

Before everyone left the workshop, I spoke to Destiny. We had a great conversation, and she was telling me how excited she was to read my book and how it's going to help so many people. I smiled and nodded my head, as I have always taken compliments lightly. I told her about my plans moving forward and how a book is actually not one of my focuses right now. My focus was to build an online course to help people become the hero of their life, and then I will do workshops and retreats. When I complete these goals, then I will create a book from the content of these accomplishments.

Her eyes rolled to the back of her head, her hand moved up and down as she nodded. Destiny was having a download, as she has the gift of channeling. I had witnessed her gift throughout the day during the workshop. She kept repeating, "No. No. No, that's not it. Write the book. The time is now." She opened her eyes and said with authority, "No. You should write the book first. You can do whatever you want in whatever order, but it will take longer if you delay writing this book. If you write the book first, then everything will happen much quicker for you, and you will know exactly what and how to do it when the time is right."

I thanked her and told her how much I appreciated her insight. I didn't really take what she said as something I needed to act on.

I try to live by the motto, "Be open to everything, and attached to nothing." I felt what she said, but I knew I had to internalize it more to know my next steps.

The next day I was heading back to Vegas, but before I did, I wanted to make sure I spent some more time at the beach and see the ocean again. I wanted to meditate and reflect on all my experiences during the workshop.

During my ocean-side meditation, I felt completely connected to my higher self instantly. I was still vibrating high from all the energy work I had done the previous day. After a few minutes of meditating, a voice came to me—the whisper that came to me in silence, the Inner Hero. It kept repeating phrases to me, "the hero who had to save himself, before he could change the world. Save yourself, save the world. Become the hero of your life. Uncover the Inner Hero." The phrases this voice was naming off were not just any phrases, I realized it was telling me book titles, book titles to the book that I was going to write. Then the voice said, "It's time. Today, you will write this book. The moment has come." Any time my Inner Hero speaks to me, especially with such certainty and authority, I answer, "Okay, Your will, will be done." I continued to say that I will start today as soon as I get home. Well, that was not the answer that my higher self wanted to hear. "No! You will start right now. Today is your, 'One day.'"

Instantly, I was back on the car ride to California. I had discovered something that I had never used, but had known for years. You might laugh at how slow I am with technology, but if you look at the bottom right side of your phone's keyboard when you are writing a text, there is a tiny symbol of a microphone. When you press and hold the microphone, you can speak into it and then your phone automatically translates your words into text on your phone. My parents had used this function for years, but I never cared to use it to write notes until that drive to California.

My higher self was telling me to use this function to write my book through speaking it out loud, and allowing my phone to transcribe my words. I had never thought about doing this before. I thought writing a book meant you had to physically either write the book with paper and pen, or type it. Transcribing my words into a book never crossed my mind.

For the next 12 hours, I spoke out loud into my phone about the story that you had just read. I completed the first part of the book in one day. This is proof that time is just an illusion. I never thought I had time to write a book. I thought it would take hours upon hours, months, maybe even years, but that wasn't the case. I thought, "I wrote a book in a single day."

But, when I completed writing the story of how I uncovered my Inner Hero, I realized I wanted to continue writing so that my readers had the resources and tools in order to uncover their Inner Hero.

That's what the second part of this book is about. YOU.

I had to edit and structure this first part of the book differently than how it came out during my 12-hour session. When you speak into your phone, the punctuation is off, and it may transcribe some words differently than intended, such as Inner Hero may turn into, In An Ear Hole! I went back through my notes to fix these minor errors, expanded on some details, and added more insights from the workshop. I didn't even start that process for over a month after I had completed that 12-hour session. It scared me to touch it. I didn't know what to do with it or how to proceed.

So I let it sit, until I joined a 100-Day Challenge with Impact Theory University, led by Tom Bilyeu. The challenge is a safe space to create a big goal, and have others be accountable, and to be empowered to actualize the goal that was important to the members.

There were 550 people at this challenge and they separated us into 44 smaller teams. I was one facilitator of one group. One thing that I have learned about taking on a leadership role is that I become a better version of myself during the process, since I believe to be a leader you must walk the talk. Everyone that joined this challenge had different goals in mind. Some were physical or health oriented, some were monetary, some based around business, relationships, education, and some much more. My goal was to finish writing this book and get it ready for the publishing process.

I thought since I had basically written the first part in one day, my goal for the second part would be easy as pie. All I would have to do is add punctuation, change some wording, and I'm done. Well, I went from 24,000 words to 87,000. I had so much more to write than I thought. Within that 100-Day Challenge, I went through many difficulties, as life was happening to me, forcing me to adapt and evolve at a quicker pace. Before I get into that, allow me to move back in time to speak about what progressed after the workshop.

A few weeks following the workshop and that 12-hour session that was seemingly a blur, I felt amazing. I felt empowered and more like myself than I had felt in a long time, if ever. I have always thought that was an interesting concept when people said, "I feel like myself more than I ever have." If you have never felt that way, then how do you know it's you? What I believe the phrase means is that they are aligned with their Inner Hero or higher self. This is our true nature, and that's why we feel more like ourselves. We feel whole in this state of consciousness.

I felt like I had received so much healing from the workshop and I spent more time out in nature, writing, and meditating. When I spoke to my friends, family, and strangers, it felt as if I could see them for who they were. I could see into them. I could see their Inner Hero as they spoke to me, and I spoke to them from that same place.

For example, my relationship with my parents has dramatically improved within the year since COVID-19 hit the world. I went to visit them weekly, bringing Greyson along so that he could bond with his grandparents. My mother and I have had tremendous growth in our relationship towards the differences in our outlook on spirituality, accepting one another's point of view with love. My father and I have become best friends. I say this to you with tears in my eyes. My father is my hero. He would humbly say that he has done nothing to deserve such a title, but through my hardships, he has held space where I felt safe, held, loved, challenged, encouraged, and free from judgement. I know I couldn't have evolved these relationships without the internal work and forgiveness that I had to go through in the previous years. I used to blame them for the traumas that I experienced as a child, without the understanding that they were doing the best that they could based on their own personal life traumas and experiences. They were just people being people. When I became a father, I understood this on a deeper core level, and changed my perspective to see them for the beautiful, selfless humans they are. I disconnected from them being my parents, which resulted in no longer seeking their approval, love, or recognition, but developing a relationship of acceptance. I received all that I once desired from them when I let it go.

When I feel I'm in alignment and flow with life, synchronicities show themselves to me consistently. Synchronicities are always around us, but we aren't in the state of consciousness to recognize them. When I'm in flow, I'm able to witness them at every moment.

For more than a year, my father and I spoke about going to a restaurant that was close to my house. Every time that we tried to go, something came up. It just wasn't the right time. A few weeks after the workshop, we could finally make time to go to this restaurant. I made a reservation for four of us, as this was the maximum number of people that could sit at a single table during 2020. Myself, Greyson, my father, and mother all went to dinner at this local neighborhood Italian restaurant, La Strega. We sat down and my mom looked around for her scarf. She believed that she may have left it in my car. I said I'd go check. Walking out of the venue, someone's sweater catches the corner of my eye. I thought nothing of it at first, but while I was walking to my car, my mind couldn't let go of the uniqueness of that sweater. I realized I had seen that sweater before, that Mackenna had that same sweater, which she received as a gift from her cousin. I thought, "That's a funny coincidence." Then I tried to think back to what else this person was wearing and realized that the yoga pants the girl at the bar was wearing were also the same yoga pants that Mackenna would often wear. Then it overcame me. "Was that Mackenna? Fuck, there's no way. Ugh. Oh man, I bet that was her." I hadn't seen or spoken to her since we broke up, and now the table where my family was sitting was facing the bar where Mackenna was sitting.

I'm not the type of person who runs away from awkward moments, so I knew when I walked back in I had to say "hi". My mom's scarf was in the car, so I grabbed it. When I walked back into the restaurant, I went straight up to Mackenna and said hello, introduced myself to her cousin, and then told her to enjoy her dinner. I sat back down at the table with my family and my mom was freaking out, "Oh my gosh, is that Mackenna? What are the odds? Do we need to leave? Is this too weird for you?" I laughed, and said, "This is exactly how the universe works. Of course she is here right now at this exact moment when we are here."

Then an old coworker and friend walks up to greet us as our server for the night. With excitement, he innocently said, "Hey, Jon. What's going on? How is Mackenna doing? She couldn't make it tonight?" I laughed again. "Funny enough, we are not together anymore, but she still made it tonight." I directed my eyes to the bar. "She's sitting right over there." I could see the horrified look on his face even through his face mask. "Oh dang. I'm so sorry, man. What are the odds of that?" I smiled at him and answered, "That's just how the universe works."

I made it through dinner, even though most of our conversations were directed towards Mackenna and me, and all the realizations that I had received about our relationship now that we weren't together. She came over to say hello to my parents and Greyson before she left. I could tell that she was on the verge of tears in this interaction, as I was also on the verge of tears throughout our dinner. I could barely focus as my heart felt overwhelmed and my gut was heavy. When I got home, Mackenna and I began to message each other about how fucking nuts it was that we ran into each other. We decided it was finally time to meet up and have closure on our relationship.

•

We met up the next night, and we spent a few hours together speaking our truths. I told her all of my realizations and took responsibility for my part in the failure of our relationship, and she did the same. We both got the closure we were looking for, yet it didn't make us feel better. I felt worse. The next day, she came over again. This time, the energy between us felt different. The previous day, Mackenna was cold emotionally. She was on a mission to speak her truth, and to be strong by not wanting to show her hurt and pain. Now she was open, soft, and loving. We spent hours talking about the life lessons we received during our time apart. Mackenna was going through the same type of internal growth I was experiencing. I felt so connected and drawn to her. It appeared, within our hearts, as a magnet, pulling toward each other. The pull was overwhelming. The desire was raw, and the love that we were withholding was now present. We craved each other's being, and we could not let that craving go unsatisfied. Mackenna and I spent the night together talking and intimately connecting. It was divine timing. Greyson was going to be on vacation with his mother for the next few days, so we ran away.

We went to the snow, spending the next three days in a small city in Utah, falling in love all over again from this new place of self-love at the core. We explored Zion, rolled around in the sheets of a tiny motel, and laughed more than we ever had before. This was the most raw and honest we have ever been with one another, sharing our fears, expressing our desires, shedding tears, and creating magical moments where time just stopped.

The relationship that we once had died, and now we had the opportunity we both desired, free from worry, fear, and doubt. Since then, we have been inseparable, and more in love. This has only been possible through the way we have learned to love ourselves, and honor each other to fill our own cup first before trying to fill up each other, and also knowing that it is OUR job to fill up our cup, and not our partner's job.

For the first time in our relationship, we talked about marriage and having kids. We couldn't stop talking about it. Every day, we talked about kids' names and what life will look like when we expand our family. Greyson was so excited to have her back in our life and it seemed like he didn't skip a beat. Everything was absolutely perfect.

We read relationship books and did the exercises together to strengthen our connection. We were spending most of our time on vacation, and not in Vegas, which was something that I wasn't interested in doing before because I was so consumed in creating a successful business.

Before our reunion, I decided that my New Year's Mantra would be, "Do less, receive more." This was all about focusing my energy on what was most important to me, rather than spreading my energy too thin. Doing less of busy work and false accomplishments, while receiving more abundance and blessings in the areas I valued most. This was me making space for my happiness, my family, my relationship with Mackenna, and my internal healing.

On Valentine's Day 2021, we found out some news that was going to shift our life forever. We had already spent 25 days out of the first 45 days of the year traveling. We were in Durango, Colorado with my parents, Greyson and my nephew. It was our last day before we were returning to Vegas. Mackenna had been feeling off for the last week, and she decided she wanted to take a pregnancy test. It so happened that the love that we had been sharing with each other was the love that creates new life. Mackenna was pregnant. We were going to be parents to a beautiful baby and Greyson was going to be a big brother. We shared the news with my family and everyone before we left the Airbnb, and we were all overwhelmed with joy and gratitude.

•

This is what synchronicities mean: the universe's ultimate alignment to one's desire. Sometimes we don't see why things work out the way they do, but perhaps it's because there is something bigger at work behind the scenes. I like to use this painting analogy often. If you were to stand two inches away from a painting, you would only see fragmented pieces, random colors blurred together, and it would seem chaotic. If you take ten steps back from this same painting, everything becomes clear to you. You see the bigger picture at hand. You realize that this painting is not random, nor chaotic, but a beautiful masterpiece perfectly constructed. This is the work that is always going on in our lives if we allow it to go through the process needed for our highest growth and purpose. Life is a beautiful masterpiece when you can zoom out and see the pieces connect perfectly.

Mackenna and I needed to allow our old relationship to die, as that version of us could not and would not allow new life. As soon as we could evolve into a new relationship, we created space for life to happen. Our baby asked us to heal before he showed up in our lives. This is the work, this is the process, this is faith, this is the perfect timing of the universe, this is the expansive creation that God has for each of us. Zoom out, and know that your Inner Hero is guiding you to your ultimate dream life.

We both were beyond excited, but we also had an overwhelming amount of fear attached to being parents. During this same time, I was facilitating my team in the 100-Day Challenge at Impact Theory University. I was also adjusting to this new reality. Upon receiving this news, Mackenna and I also received stress. This stress was reminding us of how we react during hard times. The old patterns crept in as Mackenna shut down, and I picked up drinking on a more consistent basis. Mackenna could no longer turn to alcohol or weed, but I was doing it enough for the both of us.

As I have said, we go in and out of an enlightened state of being. Fortunately, I was still living within the framework of "Do less, receive more." I continued to write every day, focusing all of my energy on this book while eliminating all other distractions, such as coaching and creating YouTube content. I showed up weekly within my group calls, trying to lead to the best of my ability, knowing that I was accountable to people other than myself. I was reflecting so much during this time, because writing this book has brought up old trauma and patterns, forcing me to look within for the lessons that I have already learned. With this reflection brought even more healing. By recognizing my patterns from the past, I could identify the ones I was reliving in the present moment, and it allowed me to adjust appropriately.

•

By taking full accountability of my triggers, I adjusted my eating habits, drank less, paid off $60K of debt, and my relationships are thriving. Mackenna and I are engaged. I wake up practicing yoga most mornings, and I wrote this book. When I could let go of the attachments that separated me from aligning with my Inner Hero fully, everything fell easily into place. "Do less, receive more."

When my energy shifted, Mackenna's energy shifted. I had to break my self-sabotaging cycle for her to break hers. I have been able to bridge the gap in between my spurts of enlightenment. This is the work, bridging the gap between who you are today, and your future IDEAL self, and this is what it means to align with your Inner Hero.

This book shows you how messy it looks when you are standing two inches away from every experience in life only to see chaos and disorder, while knowing at the same time you are actually creating a perfect masterpiece ,when you take a moment to zoom out and see the process play out. The journey that we all are embarking on is not to learn anything, but to remember the truth of what we already know. It is more of an uncovering process, removing the layers of illusions and false identities. Are we looking at shadows in our cave, or are we seeing with conscious eyes?

I could never have written this book before now. I could not tell you about the struggles I have lived, as I was too busy trying to live up to a perfect person. I could not tell you I was $60K in debt and one signature away from signing for bankruptcy because I was ashamed. I didn't want to say it out loud to the world that I was broken, because a life coach has life figured out. I felt embarrassed to tell people I had a drinking problem because I was too busy having fun, lying to myself about having the drinking under control. I wouldn't admit that for most of my life, I hated myself while I was preaching self-love.

This journey is not over for me, and it's not over for you. No matter where you are today, how old, how hard life is, how broken and unworthy you may feel, it's never too late to decide to live a different life. "It's Still Your Mother Fucking Set!"

Your body is designed to heal. You are meant to be at peace. We are born to love. We are limitless and abundant in goodness. You were born perfect and will die perfect. This is Truth. I want to give you permission. Perhaps I might be the first person to offer you permission. I want you to let that truth sit inside your heart. I want you to feel it to the core of your being. You can't do anything more to earn this truth. You don't have to be any other version than the one that you are right now. This truth is your birthright, and I give you permission to receive it.

I also give you permission to ask more about yourself and the life you are living. You can have outrageous dreams and desires and be happy. You don't have to continue to experience the reality you are living in today. It can change if you wish it to change, but you have to allow yourself to let go of the old, outdated version of you, remove the layers of doubt, limiting beliefs, self-hate, resentment, and judgment. You must forgive, forgive others, and forgive yourself. You must stop listening to the news, social media, people who hate, discourage, and manipulate. You must uncover what exists below the surface, and keep uncovering the part of yourself that has been with you from the beginning, the part of yourself that will not leave or forsake you. It is your best friend, your guardian angel, your spirit guide, your ancestors, and your higher and best self. It is the whisper behind your thoughts, the warmth in your heart, the observer of your dreams, the lover that longs for you; it is unconditional love, the creator of all that is, and intimately knows you down to every cell in your body. It knows all of your desires and the exact path to arrive at those desires.

If I can do it, I know you can do it too.

Are you ready? Are you open? Are you willing?

Your time is now, or else you wouldn't be here. It's time to uncover the Inner Hero. What is it you need to let go of or address within yourself to align with this bigger part?

As this was the story of my process of uncovering. The next part of this book is for YOU to uncover your personal Inner Hero by developing your internal superpowers.

Now that you know you are not alone, what are you going to do? Own your life and intentionally create something truly magical.

Are you going to be courageous enough to step up? I have faith that you will, and for that, I'm proud of you. Be light, love yourself, and actualize your full potential. You are a fucking badass, and it's time for you to embrace it. Let no one, especially yourself tell you anything different. You are The Hero that you have been looking for. Let's uncover it together.

PART 4

MANIFESTING YOUR
ULTIMATE POTENTIAL

CHAPTER 19
THE PROCESS
OF BECOMING

If I gave you anything in the first part of the book, it was the understanding that there is no right way to embark on your journey. There is no rulebook to tell you what to do or how to do it. My journey was far from perfect. That shit was messy. It still is.

Yet, every experience brought me here, where I am more myself than I have ever been. I have uncovered my Inner Hero, and have been aligning daily with that higher part of myself. In hindsight, I wouldn't change a thing. I see that perhaps it all was perfect, and how it was supposed to be, or else it would have been different.

The only thing that exists in this universe is a process, a process of what? A process of becoming. Becoming what, though? This is where we get to choose what we are becoming, and if we don't consciously choose what that becoming is, then the universe or society will choose for us.

I have been undergoing this process to become who I am today, and I'm still in this process, an infinite process, always evolving, and endlessly becoming the next version of myself with each new moment. I am on the leading edge of my becoming, and the same goes for you.

You have also been on a journey, whether you are aware of it or not. You have been travelling through a process of becoming, and now you are here. Think about it for a moment. Did you show up at this moment in space and time as you are today? Think back to what needed to happen in the process of life to get you here today. Don't rush, stop reading, close your eyes and reflect.

Becoming you is an infinite process. It started as far back as the existence of time. It's taken the universe billions of years to get you to where you are today. Think back to what type of perfection it took for each of your ancestors to come together in order to produce life.

It's a slow and rigorous process of becoming. Nature rushes nothing, yet it has arrived, and is perfect as it is. What did it take for your parents to come together on a microscopic level to fertilize a single egg so that you could exist? What has happened since then? Was it the process of becoming? You didn't pop out of your mom running around and talking. You had to go through learning, developing, falling down, and standing back up. It's a messy process, yet nature rushes nothing. Yet YOU have arrived, and YOU are perfect. You are nature, and the Inner Hero is your Inner Nature. Trust the process, as it is the only thing that exists in this universe. The rest of this book is about the process of becoming by uncovering your Inner Hero.

I have developed 18 Internal Powers we were all born with. The more we embody and deliberately develop these powers through a process, the more they become superpowers, which will align you with your Inner Hero. This is the process of becoming the hero in your life. Are you ready?

There are four pillars in receiving a Transformational AHA. For this transformation to be sustainable, you must keep two beliefs at the forefront of your mind because they work hand in hand. "Do the work, because the work works," alongside "The only thing that exists in this universe is a process of becoming, so trust that you are becoming, that which you have desired."

These two beliefs must be within each pillar and experienced within each superpower.

Why are these two beliefs so important you may ask? If you look back at my journey, there were many times where everything in my life felt like it was falling apart. There were so many moments where I thought maybe I was crazy, maybe I should give up on this dream, maybe I should move on. My life was crashing down right in front of my eyes, and it all started when I decided I was going to plant the seeds of creating a better life. Why then, was my life in chaos and in ruins, rather than getting better? It was because the outdated version of Jonathon had to die. It literally felt like death. I needed to grieve, and within that place I was planting new seeds. I had to let go of what I thought I was, so I could become what I had asked for.

First, what seeds are you planting?

You don't plant the seeds of a rosebush and expect apples to grow. The universe produces the fruits of the seeds you plant. Also, there is a gestation process that needs to happen when planting seeds. You wouldn't plant the seeds of an apple tree, then hope that the next day a full grown and fruitful apple tree in the backyard will appear. Both scenarios are silly, yet this is what we expect from ourselves when we decide to plant seeds of growth, prosperity, and abundance for our life. Did you plant the right seeds to bear this type of fruit? Do you understand that there is a process at work behind the scenes? The universe will follow through with the seeds that you plant, but you must be patient.

Second, do the work, because the work works.

Little did I know that this is part of the process for me to become who I had desired, and if I had given up, then I wouldn't be here today. Instead of giving up, I kept doing the work, and the more I did the work by embodying everything I was learning, the work continued to work. Do the work, because the work works.

Wanting more out of life is great, but if you do nothing about it, then how can anything change? You must decide what seeds to plant. I recommend planting the seeds that bear the fruit of your future ideal self, through which you are the hero. This looks different for everyone, and I'll be guiding you through a process later on to gain clarity about what that may look like for you.

After planting the seeds of how you envision your future ideal self, you must do the work, and allow nature to do its part. If you sit and stare at the ground after you plant the seed, it doesn't matter how much faith you have in that seed to grow, nothing will happen with faith alone.

There is work to be done, and this is part of the process. You must water the seed through your daily routine, and pull any weeds that are invading the integrity of the growth through your mind, heart, and spirit, and send loving energy to the fruit from this tree; prune back the tree after it sprouts, and make sure that it's receiving the light. If you are doing the work, then the work will work, as there is a process that is happening behind the scenes.

You are not forcing the seed to blossom into a tree. Imagine if you did and how much work that would take. You would have to break out of that tiny shell of a seed; spread roots deep into the earth in order to have a strong foundation; find your way through the soil to seek your truth out of the ground; soak up the water; absorb the sunlight; fight out the viruses and weeds of your environment; grow branches; make those branches grow more branches; develop leaves; undergo the seasons of weather; then finally bear fruit.

While that is happening, parasites, bugs, animals, and birds are trying to take the fruit that you worked so hard to produce. If you had to do all of that work, would you want to be an apple tree? Probably not! From the outside, the work that nature is doing while we are sleeping is effortless. Again, there is a gestation period between the seed and the fruitful apple tree, as there is a gestation period between planting the seeds of your desires, and then the receiving of all that you have asked for. "Do the work, because the work works," and "The only thing that exists in the universe is a process of becoming, so trust that you are becoming, that which you have desired."

Your inner nature and outer nature are also within the process and are infinitely doing the work. You can either trust and work alongside that nature, or you can deny it and work against it. Either way, you will become something. If you are aware of this process within yourself, then you get to choose what that becoming will be.

CHAPTER 20
THE 4 PILLARS OF A
TRANSFORMATIONAL AHA!

Pillar #1: Impacting Your Mind

The mind is the most powerful machine in the universe.

Perception, knowledge, and self-awareness are three areas that impact the mind.

Being open to different perspectives can influence how you see your external and internal world. The mind creates the reality that you are experiencing. Even though we both live on planet Earth, your mind is creating a distinct reality from what my mind is creating. Perception is reality, so if we change the lenses through which we see the world, then the world will inevitably change. It is law. You may change your lenses at any point. It doesn't matter if you have seen yourself in a certain way your whole life, if your perception is in any way disempowering, then put on lenses that someone else may have that would be more empowering for what you are looking to accomplish.

Knowledge is power? Wrong. Knowledge is only potential power. There are more people in the world that have more knowledge than the most successful and happiest people on earth. We must combine knowledge with self-awareness, integration, and trusting the process.

If you want to transform your life, you must take time to learn and develop your mind. Information is a powerful tool to open up new realities of possibilities. We only know what we know, so if we can expand on that, then we have more knowingness at our disposal.

Knowledge can come in different forms. Sometimes it's learning new concepts or ideas about life and how it works. Maybe it's science or different belief systems. The most important knowledge that you can learn though, is knowledge about yourself. Remember the old saying, "Know thyself"? We call this self-awareness. The more you know and expand your understanding of the self, the more you transform the self.

As I say, "Do the work, because the work, works."

You must intentionally seek new information and perspectives, and then look within to understand how you can apply that new vantage point to your life. The work here is embodiment and integration. You must integrate what you learn and embody the knowledge, to understand what works and what doesn't work for your dreams and desires. There is a big difference in conceptually knowing something that you learn and BEING what you learn. Being is the embodiment of what you know. For example, I might know what it means to express forgiveness and all of its benefits, but until I embody forgiveness, I can't know how impactful it is, or receive its benefits. Knowledge is separate from us until integrated or embodied within—then it is KNOWING.

Your life changes once the mind is impacted. You can learn a new skill set to change your career, or get promoted so you can earn more or feel more fulfilled. You can learn unique skills to save a life when someone gets hurt on a hike, or impact lives through improved communication skills, or be a better parent or spouse through learning patience.

Learning something and embodying it to a deep knowing takes time, so it's important to trust the process of the gestation period. You don't become a great communicator, coach, or business owner overnight. It takes practice and time to become that version of yourself. Trust in the process and do the work, because the work works.

Pillar #2: Emotional Impact

An emotional impact can change your life instantaneously by changing the dynamic of your vibrational frequency. An emotional impact may happen in two different ways. The first way could be from trauma, such as when Michael died. My life changed in a single moment from this deep emotional experience. It may be a diagnosis of a terminal illness, losing a job, divorce, or a near death experience. This is an emotional impact from a perceived negative experience. This can shift someone into a complete life changing positive projection or a downward spiral.

You may also experience an emotional impact from powerful positive experiences such as traveling to a different country, skydiving, psychedelics, getting married, having a child, going to a retreat, getting the job that you have always wanted, or having a profound metaphysical experience. This is when something positive happens and affects you on a deep emotional level that causes you to see life through different lenses.

Both impacts can project you toward living a more full and empowered life if you follow the flow of your Inner Nature, because it moves you dramatically outside of your comfort zone. This is where the magic lives. Another way of saying it, is that this type of experience disrupts the customary vibrational reality and shifts your base frequency. Think of it as an earthquake taking place in your vibrational field, and in doing so, the foundation of how you perceive reality moves.

For many people though, after one of these earthquakes, the emotion heightens for a brief period but subsides to the old version. You see this often with people who go to live events to see great influencers, such as Tony Robbins, Gary V, or Grant Cardone. People receive a massive motivational high after leaving these events, almost vibrating, experiencing a powerful emotional impact. They are feeding off of the speakers' energy and the other people in the audience, who are also on a high. When getting home, there is a feeling like they can do anything. They have the answers to life figured out, and then want to tell the entire world what they have experienced.

Some people create sustainable change from these events through integrating what they have learned, but most of the people attempt to live off of that high, and lose that high after a few weeks because they don't continue to fan the flame that ignited them. They get back into an old environment, with old friends, with old routines, and old energy. It's no wonder they don't create sustainable change and move back into their previous vibrational reality, as that is where their foundational set point is familiar.

This is where we water that seed, fan that flame, and build upon the new foundation introduced to us in these potential life-changing experiences.

It's important to move outside of your comfort zone. By doing this, you will inevitably receive more emotional impacts, as the unknown brings in the magic of new life. New vibrational frequencies change your average set point. Putting yourself into these uncomfortable situations is part of doing the work under this pillar.

By being open to vulnerability in these uncomfortable experiences, you will also have a deep impact on your emotional state. Trusting that the unknown, and everything that you are looking for is outside of your comfort zone is a crucial aspect of growth. If what you wanted existed in your comfort zone, then you would already have it. New things bring new experiences, which bring in new opportunities, which bring in new emotions. This process changes your vibrational reality.

Pillar #3: Collective Impact

We are not meant to do this journey alone. We have been tribal beings since the beginning of time. We have all heard of the saying that we are the average of the five people we spend the most time with. Who are the five people that you spend your time with? Has this list changed in the last five years? If not, I would guess your life has changed little in the last five years.

Our environment has a massive effect on our energy and the results we receive in life. I talked about how people receive an emotional impact while attending retreats and live events. They leave these events experiencing a high cleaner than any drug, and it feels as if they are levitating. I have felt this many times after a workshop, event, or a retreat. This happens because we are in a new environment with new people who have huge dreams and desires.

These are like-minded people who are at these events to change their lives. The collective energy and environment influence your experience and your vibrational field, heightened and elevated through the power of the collective. That fire ignites from within during the experience, but if they do not fan the flame, the fire will burn itself out.

How do you fan the flame? This is the work. You must plug yourself into different tribes and communities that have the desire to bear the same type of fruit you want. Some people in this ecosystem may be at the beginning of planting their seeds, while others have been bearing the fruits for their labor for years. You are surrounding yourself with people who have similar ambitions and desires as you. You must put yourself out there to meet new people and wet your feet in different communities to see what feels the best, to find a group of people where you feel safe to dream ridiculously big dreams. They hold you accountable, and who are rooting for you to succeed.

When you can find these types of people, you begin to collectively impact each other and you elevate to the next version of yourself. Surround yourself with people who think, feel, believe, and behave within an empowering reality. By being around energy that is expansive and growth oriented, you will be expansive and growth oriented. Remember to share your success and ideas with everyone. You never know who is seeking a new tribe, but needs the permission to dream and put themselves out there. You could be that person.

Even when you find yourself a tribe that you connect to, remember to keep testing the waters. The more diverse communities you involve yourself with, the more knowledge you receive, the more variety of perspectives you gain, and the more you move into uncomfortable experiences. This is a process that never ends, so do the work, because the work, works.

Pillar #4: Impact of Repetition

We are who we are today because of the impact of repetition. I remember watching my son learning how to walk. He didn't start walking on day one. He first had to learn how to hold his head up, to learn how to roll over, then crawl, then stand up using the countertop or couch. I would sit him in his bouncy so that his legs would grow stronger. Eventually, he would start standing up without help. He would build some balance and confidence to take a step. Of course, he would fall down, not once, or twice, but hundreds of times for a few months. He never gave up, though. It wasn't an option. Finally one day he started walking. He didn't stop with that accomplishment. He kept moving, getting better and better with walking until it turned into running, climbing, and jumping. It was amazing to watch, yet as adults we walk with ease and think nothing of it.

We tend to not pay attention to the power of repetition and practice. The only reason we are who we are today is because we have repeatedly thought the same thoughts, perceived the same perceptions, believed in the same beliefs, felt the same emotions, and behaved within the same behaviors through repetition. We become what we repeatedly do. A favorite quote of mine is by Annie Dillard, "How we spend our days is, of course, how we spend our lives." We repeat each day without observing much change. This may seem like a bad thing, but what if we could reprogram our days? That seems pretty promising, right? Well we can, but we need to understand who we are looking to become.

Let's go back to our seed analogy. What type of seed did you plant? This will determine what you would like to repeat. It doesn't matter where you are today. As I've said, the only thing that matters is where do you want to go, and who are you willing to become to get there?

Our brain lives on repeat for efficiency. It takes a lot of energy to think about every move, every thought, and to choose every decision that needs to be made. This efficiency is part of the design and is here to work for us, not against us. At first, repetition seems like a lot of work, because you are used to engaging in life specifically, and now you are disrupting the efficiency that was created. Think of it this way, when you look at the Grand Canyon, you are in awe of its beauty. It took an unimaginable amount of time for a stream of water to carve into the rocks to create this sight of beauty.

Our brain works similarly, where we have neural pathways, mini carved out rivers in our brain, sending signals everywhere in our body. These signals design our life, and tell us what to think, how to feel, how to react to certain stimuli, and a billion other things that are beyond our knowledge. Default carved these brain pathways out over time, mostly through the environment. We can carve out new rivers into our brain, but it takes some time, as it took time to get you to where you are today.

Science says it takes 21 days to create a habit. I believe it takes more than DOING something repeatedly for you to get the results that you are looking for. The goal is to BE what you do, rather than do what you do. The version you see yourself to be in the future is WHO YOU ARE, not what you do, and that takes longer than

21 days. This is a lifestyle change, which is deeper than repeatedly performing a habit.

Repetition is a process, and you must do the work, because the work works. This means, you must journal about who you desire to be, and develop clarity in how that future ideal version of yourself thinks about himself, talks to herself, what she believes in, what he does daily, how he treats other people, what she does for a living, and on and on. By finding clarity on what it means to be the hero of your life, then you can start understanding how you take the first step in bridging that gap. When you understand this, and intentionally engage with the first three pillars, you will receive a Transformational AHA! This last pillar may be the most important, because you must consistently use repetition in each pillar in order to embody the Inner Hero.

Repetition seems tedious, but one day you will wake and realize you have BECOME the desired version of yourself. Yet remember, the only thing that exists in the universe is the process, and we never finish. A process of what? A process of becoming. It is never ending, and it's a limitless becoming. We choose what that becoming is, or it chooses to become for us. Practice repeating, as if you already are the hero of your life, and let go of everything that doesn't align with that version. This is how we carve new neural pathways that align with our desired self.

Reminder. Each one of these pillars can create change in your life, but repeatedly integrating all four within each of the Superpowers will create sustainable and lasting change. This is a Transformational AHA!

One day you will wake up, and say, "I have arrived."

You will no longer feel you are ACTING like someone you desired to be years prior, but you ARE that person. This is what it feels like to be aligned with your Inner Hero. This is the nature of transformation. Remember to trust the process, and do the work, because the work, works.

CHAPTER 21
UNCOVERING YOUR INNER HERO

I have provided the first pillar of impact so you may receive a Transformational AHA! I hope to have affected your mind through perception, knowledge, and self-awareness by having you reflect on the way we have constructed reality. The rest of this book is experiential and interactive. I empower you to engage with these superpowers through journaling, reflecting, and embodying them.

There is a massive opportunity for you to transform your life and wake up to the potential inside that has been lying dormant. This may be an easy transformation to becoming the hero of your life, or it may be the hardest thing you have ever gone through—but remember, you are not alone. Look back at my story, and how messy it was, and yet I have been able to become the best version of myself, because I didn't give up. I trusted the process, and I repeatedly did the work.

I would like to tell you that who I am today, is far beyond what I could have ever imagined, but that wouldn't be true. I imagined this version first, before I could become it. This is just the beginning. I have imagined so much more for myself in the lifetime to come, and I am practicing being that version every day by aligning with my Inner Hero. I know you are ready for this transformation. I believe in you. Do you believe in yourself?

•

I give you permission to let go of any limiting beliefs. You don't need them anymore. You are in a safe space to dream bigger than you have ever dreamed, because you are a dreamer.

I give you permission to ask more of yourself, and hold yourself at a higher standard, as we aren't meant to just dream; but instead meant to actualize our dreams by tapping into our full potential. I give you permission to be scared, because change is scary; permission to let go, because whatever you have been holding on to has been holding you back.

I give you permission to be excited, because life SHOULD be exciting. I give you permission to have fun with this, or else what's the point? I give you permission to be uncomfortable, as what we want does not exist in our comfort zone. I give you permission to want more out of life, because we can be, do, and have anything we desire. I give you permission to be happy, because this is the ultimate gift of life. I give you permission to not feel guilty, it's okay to evolve. I give you permission to take accountability for your life, as you are the creator and no one else is. I give you permission to let go of shame, as the past is behind you, to become the hero of your life, because that is the truth of your inner nature.

•

How you maximize the rest of this book.

As you have learned, The Impact of Repetition is one of the most important pillars to receive a Transformational AHA! It does not mean the superpowers listed below should be reviewed just one time. They are to be reviewed endless times, month after month, year after year. The more you learn this information, the more you embody these superpowers, then the more you will become aligned with your Inner Hero. Again, do the work, because the work works. This is becoming the hero of your life. These will be the tools and concepts to help you BE that version of yourself.

There are 18 Internal Powers. We are born with these powers, as these powers are not external abilities or skill sets, but internal values and faculties of the mind, heart, and spirit, innate to us all. Note that I said these are "powers" and not "superpowers." We must learn how to develop and embody these powers for them to become superpowers, or else these powers will lie dormant inside of you.

In any superhero movie, when the hero discovers their powers, they are simply powers. Superman hears everyone's thoughts. He can't fly, he doesn't know his strength, but with time and practice, he develops them into superpowers. He first had to recognize his abilities, understand them, and believe that he could improve them to a higher level. This is what I encourage you to do, recognize that you have these powers, understand the full potential of them, believe that you have the potential to improve them, and repeatedly develop them. The more and more you do this the more and more you will uncover the Inner Hero.

You may go at your own pace, but I don't recommend blazing through the rest of this book; but taking on one power at a time, and diving deep into what it means for you when you integrate that power into your life.

I encourage you to journal about the insights you receive with each Superpower and how they show up in your life. Look for opportunities throughout the day to see how you can apply and develop each of these powers into your routine.

Join the Discord community *A Hero's Academy* and share your insights. Again, in Pillar 3, Collective Impact is important to receive a Transformation AHA! Engage in the community and find others who are on a similar journey.

How you proceed is up to you, but I ask that you do the work, because the work, works. Making these powers super is up to you, and no one can do the work for you. The process of becoming belongs to you and you alone. I'm here to guide you and empower you.

Are you ready?

Before diving into the superpowers, stop what you are doing, get out a piece of paper, and title it at the top, "My Transformational AHA!"

Let's set some intentions. Take a moment and visualize yourself completing the rest of this book. You embraced and embodied the teachings of each of the 18 superpowers. You continue to review them, journaling about new awareness and insights you are receiving. You begin to change your thoughts, beliefs, the way you see yourself, and how you show up in life. You began to implement the superpowers into your daily awareness. Fast forward one month. You've received a miraculous internal shift. You received a Transformational AHA! What was the miraculous transformation you received?

Write in as much detail as you can. What challenges have you overcome? In what areas did you receive any epiphanies? What have you been manifesting? What are the quality of the thoughts you have been experiencing? How have you been feeling emotionally by implementing these new superpowers into your life?

Be sure to write as if it already has happened. You are reflecting in hindsight by looking backwards. Have fun with this exercise and be sure to not hold anything back. Dream big. Use the gift of a childlike imagination. You can receive ANY miracle that you want. Let's see your creativity shine!

Congratulations! You are now ready to move forward.

Keep your journal handy. At the end of each superpower, I will prompt you with a question to reflect upon. This is part of doing the work.

INTERNAL SUPERPOWERS

I've grouped the superpowers into six Segments.

Awakening To Your Inner World: The Foundations Of Change

    1. Own Your Reality

    2. Self-Awareness

    3. Intentionality

    4. Self-Talk

The Lenses Of The Mind

    5. Perception

    6. Appreciation

    7. Visionary

Having Purpose

    8. Spirituality

    9. Drive

    10. Leadership

Uncovering The Inner Hero: Your True Nature

    11. Love

    12. Forgiveness

Aligning With The Inner Hero

    13. Embodiment

    14. Integrity

    15. Faith

Being The Inner Hero

    16. Attitude

    17. Connection

    18. Opportunist

CHAPTER 22

SUPERPOWERS 1-4

AWAKENING TO YOUR INNER WORLD:

THE FOUNDATIONS OF CHANGE.

Awakening to your inner world: The foundations of change

It's not about how wide you live, but how deep. The deeper you reflect, develop, and embody these internal superpowers, the fuller your life will be.

This first segment awakens you to your inner world. Most people don't change their life unless something externally happens, causing them to react in a way that makes them want to change. The external event could be one of the two emotional impacts that we talked about earlier. Perhaps it's less dramatic; they don't fit in their jeans anymore, or they have flies coming out of their wallet. Maybe they have been alone for a long time, and they are searching for love. They could be experiencing a midlife crisis, or they are bored, so they are looking to spice life up. Whatever it is, it's usually because something from the outside has caused them to feel a certain way, which makes them want to change.

The way you sustain change comes from your inner world. Most people hope that something externally will be their hero, and save them. Think about it. If someone feels alone and desiring love and then gets into a relationship, they're pursuing an external hero to save them. They hope the person will help them feel loved, and not alone. This works for only a brief period until they feel alone within the relationship, and complain about their partner not loving them. This happens time and time again, because this type of person thinks their partner is the problem, and so they believe the answer to this is to find another partner who will now take the place as the hero, rather than understanding it's their fault for why they feel alone and unloved.

How many people each year will set a New Year's Resolution to lose weight? A shit ton, that's how many. They buy gym memberships, healthy food and get on the newest diet trend; thinking this is the hero to their problems, but they inevitably fail for the fifth year in a row. They thought they would feel better about themselves if they lost weight by DOING the right things, but they are left feeling even shittier about themselves because they didn't lose the weight and they gave up on themselves.

People who are broke believe they would be happier and their life's problems would go away if they made more money. Yes, money is the hero for this type of person, and of course if they have more, then they will be saved; yet billionaires kill themselves. They make more money than they know what to do with, yet they suffer from the same stress, unhappiness, and unworthiness as a broken person.

Money, relationships, and body image are not our heroes, and they can't fix how we feel about ourselves within. It's an illusion. The way to change is to do the hardest work there is, which is to look within yourself, into all the dark corners and take ownership. To create sustainable change in your life, go WITHIN. There is no way around it, or you will continue to manifest the same emotional results over and over with a different picture on the screen of your mind. People might look different, the husband or wife may seem new; your career field may change, yet you felt the same way repeatedly. You get the same emotional results. When you face the root problem of these emotions from within, rather than looking for something on the outside to save you, then you can transform and release the root emotion behind all the failed attempts to change your life.

It's time to awaken to your inner world. It's time for YOU to be the hero of YOUR LIFE.

Superpower #1: Own your reality

We have all been victims in our lives. It can be as little as being a victim of someone who cuts you off in traffic and you get pissed off and flip them the bird, or as big as being raped as a child, living within fear and being unsafe in relationships for your entire adult life, and everywhere in between. The most fucked up thing about being a victim is that it's validated. It's true; someone cut you off and might drive like an asshole. It's true; some person did horrifically take your innocence away as a child. All victims feel like a victim because they were victimized, and that is a real experience.

As one of my mentors likes to say, "Now what?" You can get upset every time you get into a car, cussing out every careless driver, blaming them for why you are angry, or you can take ownership of your emotional state. Why do we behave badly when others behave badly? You got angry, not them. YOU have more than one option in how you consciously choose to respond, such as slowing down when you see a sporadic driver, and deciding to drive more cautiously while being calm and collective at the same time. You can OWN that experience and your response to it.

You may have been raped, and if so, I'm so sorry for what you went through and how it has affected your life, and your relationships. I don't want to make you feel invalidated about what happened to you, as it was completely unjustifiable. Now what? You can blame that one person, and yet, who knows what fucked up things have happened to them in their life, as they weren't always like that; reminding you there is a process of becoming for everyone.

Now what?

Is the violator the reason for the failed relationships in your life, why you feel unsafe to give yourself to someone intimately, or why you can't trust a man or woman? You have more options. Safety does not come from someone else, but from within. Own that you are the reason you feel unsafe and untrusting. Yes, it's hard, incredibly hard, and this may seem harsh and insensitive, but I promise, I love you, I care for you, and I want the best for you. Being imprisoned within that single event is hell on earth, and I empower you to release it.

Owning your reality is the only way to save yourself from any trauma you have faced. Don't allow someone to take away the rest of your life, happiness, worthiness, faith, and future relationships for something that has happened years ago. I'm not saying any of these powers we possess will easily transform into superpowers. We must look into the dark corners of our inner world and face our fears of reliving our past trauma. Maybe we need help and should go to counseling? If so, great! That is us, owning our reality.

Owning your reality means that your existence belongs to you, and you alone. By taking extreme ownership of our lives is how we transform into the hero of our lives. When you own your reality, you are no longer blaming anyone else for why your life hasn't worked out the way you had hoped. It's your fault. Yes, that hurts to admit, but it's true. It's not your fault for being victimized, but it is your fault if you stay a victim. No one can save you, and this is the first step in becoming the hero who saves themselves.

My father always told me that life is full of decisions. I only recently understood what that means. We must own each decision, and depending on the quality of that decision, will depend on the quality of our life. You must take responsibility for everything. Will you decide to stay in debt, or will you take responsibility for your finances; develop the discipline that you need to not spend money, and then save any extra money in order to pay off your debt? Maybe how you take responsibility is by learning a new skill set in which you can make more money, and stop blaming everyone else around you for why you are in debt. Can you make time to read a book or watch a YouTube video on how to create a side hustle? I'm sure you have time to watch that new Netflix series? Stop blaming others for where you are at in life, and make decisions that empower your present reality, and your future reality.

Own the fact that you can't hold a job, or why you have been in multiple failed relationships. It's not because of your boss that you keep quitting or getting fired, and it can't be the last five girlfriends' fault why the relationship ended. You are the common denominator in all of these scenarios. Let's say it was your boss's fault, or all of your girlfriends were crazy. Then that means you are making poor decisions about the jobs and partners you choose in life. Own it!

If you are not happy in life, it's your fault. I've been to poorer countries that have happy people everywhere. Take responsibility for your emotional state of being, take responsibility for your relationships, take responsibility for your finances, take responsibility for your traumas, take responsibility for the decisions you make, take responsibility for the results that you have in your life, take responsibility for EVERYTHING. If you hit rock bottom, then own it. Stop making excuses. Stop explaining the reasons you are there and why you can't get out of your current situation. Stop justifying every undesired experience you go through. This seems harsh, but you need to hear it because I doubt anybody has checked you in this area, but I'm not here to sugarcoat, I'm here to wake you the fuck up. Your existence belongs to you, and you alone. It's time to own your reality.

There's good news, though. If you take ownership of every aspect of your life and decide that it's your fault for why you are where you are now, then no one else has power over you. This is how you take back your power, and if it's your fault for all the shitty things that have happened in your life, then that also means it's your fault for all the amazing things that have happened in your life. If you are the reason you hit rock bottom, then YOU are the reason you climbed out. This doesn't mean you have to do this alone. If you need help, take ownership of that, and seek support. If you have the power to fail, then you have the power to succeed. If you take ownership of why you are poor, then you can take ownership for why you become rich.

Own your mind and what is going in and out of it. Own your heart for how it feels, your soul's purpose for what it pursues. Own your results, for it will show where you need to grow. Own your reality, or else your reality will own you. There is no other way to become the hero of your life. This is the truth of the matter. You can own it, or deny it, but you must own whatever you decide. If you can surrender to this truth, your life will change instantly. Where can you take more ownership of your life?

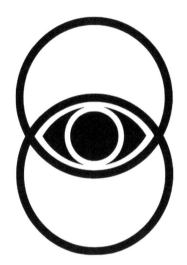

Superpower 2: Self-awareness

There is a cord that intertwines with every single one of the 18 superpowers. Without this cord, there is no way to develop an internal power. Do you know what this cord is? This is the cord of self-awareness. Awareness is the first step in transforming your life. If you don't know what to change, how do you expect it to change? If you are not aware enough to know how your thoughts influence your emotional state, how your emotional state influences your daily behaviors, and how your daily behaviors drive your results, then you will think everything that happens to you is a random occurrence. In fact, that is farthest from the truth. Here are a few scriptures and quotes shared by many teachers about our thoughts.

"As someone thinks within himself, so he is."

- Proverbs 23:7

"Do not copy the behavior and customs of this world, but let God transform you into a new person by changing the way you think. Then you will learn to know God's will for you, which is good and pleasing and perfect."

- Romans 12:2

"Be very careful about what you think, your thoughts run your life."

- Proverbs 4:23

"The mind is everything. What you think you become."

- Buddha

"Very little is needed to make a happy life; it is all within yourself in your way of thinking."

- Marcus Aurelius

This theme replays itself within the lives of people who have undergone transformation. The more aware you are, the more you can guide your life in the direction that you would like to take. Being aware of your thoughts is one area of life to be mindful of and how it affects the whole. A tool that I learned from my coaching program in iPEC helped build my awareness are the Six Energetic Influencers:

1.   Mental
2.   Physical
3.   Emotional
4.   Environmental
5.   Social
6.   Spiritual

Each of these categories has a distinct effect on your attitude, and how you show up in the world. Being self-aware in these categories and knowing where you could use some more attention can absolutely change your life. These energetic influencers are cross pollinated, as in, if one of these areas is out of balance, then it's possible that another area is also.

Allow me to go a little deeper into each area so that you can start developing your Self-Awareness into a superpower.

Mental Influencer

I started with this influencer first because we must focus on our minds as step one when creating real, lasting change. Something directly correlated to the Mental Influencer has to do with the mind, or how the mind processes one's thoughts and experiences. What is the quality of your thoughts, perception, imagination, memory, self-narrative, clarity, learning ability, and anything else that may come from the mind? Another way of saying mental influencer is mindset.

To develop awareness with your mindset, you must first think about what you think about. This sounds silly, but most of the time, thoughts pop up without us even being aware of the quality of them. Science claims we average around 70,000 thoughts a day. That is an absolutely insane amount of thoughts, and if we are lucky, we are conscious of only 5% of them. This means 95% of our thoughts are on autopilot, and are being governed by the subconscious mind. Our work in this area is to become self-aware and observe each of our thoughts, as they are right now, without changing them. We want to understand where our mindset is at, or another way to say it is, what is your mind set at? By being aware of what setting our mind is on, we can set it at the level of consciousness we desire. The more we intentionally develop the mind's set point, the more we can close the gap between the conscious and unconscious mind. It's all about mindset.

This might seem like an overwhelming amount of work to be taking notes on every thought, but let's say that all the ancient teachers were right, and thoughts do indeed create our reality. Wouldn't it be worth it to practice our proficiency at being aware of how our reality is being created, so that we can redirect it to where we want it to go?

With conscious repetition, it's only a matter of time until the quality of your thoughts elevates and shifts into the subconscious.

How do you know what thoughts need to change? Are the thoughts being experienced empowering you, uplifting you, and loving you, or are they disempowering you, limiting you, and judging you? It's time to audit your thoughts and realize how they are influencing your life. You can realize how empowering your thoughts are by looking at society, the surrounding people, the life you have manifested, and the amount of judgement you express on all of it. When you express your true thoughts about each of these subjects and how you perceive them in your mind, you will have a feeling in your body that is expansive, or contractive. This is how you realize what is empowering you and what's disempowering you. Your mind directly influences each area of your life. It's time to be honest with yourself and your mind.

The Physical Influencer

The Physical Influencer has to do with anything in relation to the body. How well can you physically express yourself in any task or action? It's easy to detect whether you have a healthy, engaged energy in this area because of how you feel and look physically. Your Physical Influencer has to do with adequate sleep, nutrition, eating habits, exercise, overall health, and the ability in which your body completes the tasks that your mind tells it too. If you have low energy in this area, you will have poor posture, be over or underweight, be tired, sick, slow, have low volume when speaking, and be lazy. Spaces in which you want to enhance your energetic engagement with your physical influencers include working out, cold showers, eating healthy, fasting, massages, chiropractic work, meditation, hiking, sleep, following through with what you say, and drinking plenty of water. The other five influencers will directly have a positive or negative effect on the physical influencer, but you can be specific in this area to see where you can improve, which can also improve your other energetic influencers simultaneously.

The Emotional Influencer

The Emotional Influencer has to do with the way you feel in relation to your emotions. With this influencer, your energy correlates with how you process the way you think about yourself, others, and experiences; which in return creates an energetic charge in your body that makes you feel a certain way, and then creates an emotional response. It's important to realize how the first two influencers, the Mental and the Physical, affect your Emotional Influencer.

To explain it further, thoughts have a specific vibrational set point, which causes a matching vibrational set point with a specific feeling in the body. Depending on the quality of the vibrational frequency of the thoughts and feelings will determine the quality of your emotional reaction. Depending on the quality of your emotion will determine the quality of your behaviors. The quality of your behaviors will determine the quality of the results you receive in life. This cycle is one of the most important cycles to become self-aware of, as your thoughts, feelings, emotions, behavior, and results will show you the quality of your life, whether it's a negative or positive charge. To make it easy to recognize, you can ask yourself in each of these areas whether you feel empowered or disempowered when you focus on them.

When this influencer is out of harmony, you will experience stress such as anger, anxiety, depression, apathy, be easily triggered, have negative self-talk, and more. When you have high engaged energy in this space, you will have emotional intelligence and awareness, clear verbal expression of how you feel, empowering self-talk; balance in your hormones, emotional stimulation such as excitement, passion, or joy; you can manage stress in a healthy way, and can provide self-love along with the capacity of loving others. Your emotional state of being is a great indicator of how satisfied you are with your life, and is a powerful tool in helping guide you in the areas that you would like to work on.

The Environmental Influencer

The Environmental Influencer associates with the setting or condition in which a particular activity is being experienced. Examples of environmental conditions would be location, temperature, lighting, cleanliness, organization, comfort of clothing, equipment or supplies for an activity, and mood of setting. It's important to be aware of how your environment makes you feel. Is your house or office cluttered or messy? If so, where else are you holding on to clutter? Where do you think and feel best? Maybe it's at the park or on a nature walk, or maybe a coffee shop with the white noise of people talking in the background? Are you wearing casual clothes when you work or do you like to look and feel professional by dressing up? Is your home life quiet and peaceful or chaotic and out of control? If your environment is not set up in the ways you are accustomed, stress can get stored in the body, keeping you from performing at an optimal level, which translates to lower energy overall. An organized environment is an organized mind. Your external environment is a mirror to your internal world.

The Social Influencer

The Social Influencer is all about your relation to family, spouse, friends, society, community, and your organization. It's how you relate to and connect with others. With a healthy and high energy in this area you will influence others and communicate effectively, have a good attitude when working with or competing with others, effect how engaged you are with your desired culture, improve the level of service you provide within your community, surround yourself with like-minded people, be accountable to others, and be more likely to experience a healthy relationship within your partnership, family, co-workers, and friends. You will feel supported by others and you will also support others healthily when having a high energy as a social influencer. When having lower energy in this area, you might experience others expressing disapproval of you or something you did, you may not be supporting others or feeling supported by them in return, you may feel smothered or drained by your relationships, have a toxic family life, and be taken advantage of or experience a drop in energy when around management or co-workers. Being aware of your Social Influencer by how you engage with others can tell you a lot about how you feel about yourself. It may show you where you are confident, or where you may be insecure. By paying attention to the quality of your relationships, you may discover some of your internal limiting beliefs. The social influencer can be a powerful mirror, uncovering immense clarity of who you are and how you relate in this world.

The Spiritual Influencer

The Spiritual Influencer is the driver for what you do. Your sense of purpose for, and meaning in, all aspects of your personal and professional life affect it. It's what is behind your sense of fulfillment and contribution to your family, community, and world. Some see this as religion, but you can be an artist and have a full spiritual connection with how it makes you feel and the way you can express yourself. When you have low energy in this area, you might experience distrust in yourself or others, and you may lack confidence. You might have no sense of purpose or goals, or you can't seem to complete any goals that you set for yourself. You may easily lose motivation. You may not have clarity in your values, feel helpless, give up when things get uncomfortable or difficult, lack awareness in most areas of life, and have no sense of direction in your subconscious mind that is driving your life.

In contrast, when you have high energy in your spiritual life, you will have purpose and direction in life. You will set goals and follow through on them, you are consciously aware of yourself and how all the other influencers affect your energy; you have faith in more than what you see with the eye. You have a sound foundation in values, and you are resilient when life gets tough. This is the most important energetic influencer because it is the core of all the other influencers. The more you get to know yourself intimately, the more you can help guide yourself to a better feeling place. I will touch more on spirituality later, and how the Inner Hero relates to it.

Journaling is one of the most powerful and efficient ways to become more self-aware. In your journal, reflect on the quality of each of the energetic influencers and how they apply in your life. How can you improve your awareness in each area?

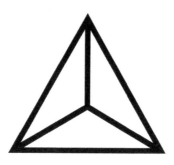

Superpower #3: Intentionality

"How you do anything, is how you do everything." I live my life by this statement. The more intentional that I am about the little things in life, the more I see the big things unfold for me in a beautiful fashion. I define intentionality as "How you deliberately choose to show up during any experience, before it happens." This is the key to having abundant success in life, whether it's regarding relationships, love, financial wealth, purpose, or having a pleasant experience at the grocery store. Deliberately creating intentions before everything that you do expands the experience and gives you an opportunity to respond the way you previously intended, rather than reacting out of impulse.

"Successful people are not successful in what they do, but how they do it." You can do all the things that a successful person does, but that doesn't mean you will find fulfillment or success. It is the intention behind what they do that makes them who they are because, "How they do anything, is how they do everything."

Creating an intention is not simply stating that you would like to workout today. Creating an intention is to contemplate an experience before it happens in great emotional detail, based on how you desire to feel during and at the end of the experience. It's making the choice before getting to the gym of what type of exercises you will do for specific parts of your body, and knowing how many sets and reps you will achieve. You will have already decided on how hard you want to work out, and how you will respond when you get tired. Are you going to give up and say that was enough for today, or will you tell yourself that you have two more sets to finish, because you are the type of person who follows through with what they say? To add to this intention, you will know the feeling that you would like to experience when you are walking out of the gym. "I feel strong and proud of myself for working out hard and finishing every exercise."

You can get as intentional as you want in any scenario. The more intentional you are, the more you have given thought to how you would like to feel and experience life. How do you want your days to look, relationships to feel, how many vacations do you want to take this year and where, what type of parent would you like to be, how much money do you want to manifest in your bank account, and the list goes on. If you want to create the life that you desire, then you must also possess an immense amount of discipline.

Discipline is a big part of staying true to your intentions. Without discipline, you may be wishy-washy in deciding, or be at the mercy of life's unexpected circumstances. You may find that a negative person can take your joy away with ease, if you are not being disciplined in your happiness. A true, joyful person will let a negative person come into their experience, and still express their happiness while allowing the other person to continue to be negative. In my experience the negative person actually becomes more joyful by the time they leave my presence, because I intentionally choose joyfulness in all of my interactions with people without trying to change anything around me, because I adjust my inner world to my intention. "Change the lens in which you see the world, and the world will change." Have you intentionally chosen the lenses through which you wish to see the world?

We can't predict or plan everything that happens in our life, but we can decide on who we are, how we would like to show up, and how we would like to feel before we manifest anything. We can choose how we would like to respond to life before it unfolds into reality. We get to choose our values and the laws in which we want to live. We get to choose to be intentional if we want, and that's a pretty amazing gift if you ask me. So let us use this gift as the power that it is, and choose to be more intentional in how we show up BEFORE we show up. This takes daily practice; so while moving forward in this book get into the habit of creating an intention before moving into each superpower.

Throughout your day, focus on making intentions. How do you think that would change the quality of your experiences? Where do you need to develop more discipline in your life?

Superpower #4: Self-talk

This is our last superpower for Awakening to your inner world: The foundations of change. If you think about it, you talk to yourself more than anyone else in the entire universe. There is constant chatter up there. Who is actually talking, and who is listening? Where is this dialog coming from, and how does it decide on where it's going?

Self-talk can literally break you, or build you up. Our words can curse our life, or bless our life. We have typically two voices in our heads speaking to us at the same time, the Inner Villain, and the Inner Hero. You have seen the scenes in the cartoons that have the devil on one shoulder while having an angel on the other. They are both speaking to the character, trying to convince them to either do something or not. This is how it works for you and I. One of those voices is there to put us down, get us into trouble, and disempower us, while the other voice is uplifting us, aligning us with our values, and wanting to empower us in everything that we engage in.

There are three tools I encourage you to focus on while you are developing this superpower.

Reframing

Reframing is when we RECREATE a narrative in our head about a person, belief, experience, idea, or concept. The story that we tell ourselves can be our best friend or worst enemy. The story is our "frame of reference." We live and die with these stories. We can use reframing in many ways.

Reframing your frame of reference

Reframing is all done in the head. By assuming or interpreting a story in your head, you must also recreate the story in your head. This is how reframing becomes a tool. When reframing as a superpower, it creates an empowering frame of reference. The stories that you tell yourself and others are uplifting and non-judging. You may reframe an experience in the past, a present scenario, or even adjust how you view a future event. You may also use reframing in how you perceive people in your life. We can use reframing in any facet of time.

For instance, a situation in the past didn't play out the way you'd hoped for. Maybe it left you feeling deflated or disempowered. Regardless of what happened or who was involved, the only thing that is continuing to hold you captive is the story you are telling yourself, and not the actual event itself. Therefore, when you go back to situations in your life that have held you captive, you can reframe the story by finding gratitude for the event (because it brought you to where you are now), or simply reframing it in your mind by how it played out and how it has benefited your life. The only person you hurt by holding on to grudges or life disasters is you.

Reframe your life and gain your power back. Most of us have experienced some sort of trauma in our past that is surrounded by a specific person or people. We could blame it on the parents, family members, friends, co-workers, bullies, teachers, or anyone else. The reason we are holding on to this specific story might be valid, but retaining it ultimately harms us.

Reframing past relationships

By being able to recreate the story you have around people in your past, you can let go, forgive, move on, and see the best in them. This is not only a very healing experience, but it also frees you from the bondage of the repeated story you have been telling your-self about this person. Sometimes, the person who you need to reframe the story around the most is the story you tell yourself about yourself.

It's common that individuals fall into a cycle of negative self-talk. It could be because of many reasons. Maybe you have high standards or are insecure. Maybe you have let yourself down or feel that you deserve it. There are plenty of other examples, but negative talk would not be acceptable if you were to speak to your friends or family in the way you speak to yourself; so change your self-talk today. Remember, you must be your number one fan. You can learn to love yourself and speak to yourself with words of empowerment and grace.

Reframing beliefs

Beliefs can either hold you captive or set you free. Sometimes we don't understand where our beliefs came from, why we believe what we do, or why we don't believe in certain things. If it doesn't give you freedom or empower you, then it's time to upgrade them through reframing.

Affirmations

Affirmations are words, statements, or phrases that you repeat to yourself about the reality you wish to embody. I see affirmations as magic spells. The magic spells or phrases that you repeat to yourself have a specific energetic charge. The more you say them and FEEL them in your body, the more you charge their vibrational currency. Another way to say that is, the more you can use affirmations, the more powerful these magical spells become.

There are many ways to use affirmations.

First, I would like you to start with a present tense power frame. "I am _____." In that blank space, you put the desired result or empowered feeling, whether or not you see it right now. "I am learning more every day." "I am trusting in the process." "I will do the work, because the work, works." "I am evolving into my Inner Hero every day." "I am healing old traumas." These are a few examples, but I would like you to create your list of affirmations that match with your desires. Another form of affirmation that Tom Bilyeu uses often is "I am the type of person that _____." Fill in the blank space with the description of the type of person you would like to embody. "I am the type of person that prioritizes my health every day." "I am the type of person that leans into hard things." "I am the type of person that sees the good in everyone." "I am the type of person that makes a positive difference in the world." Repeat the phrases that you create for yourself to yourself as many times as you can throughout the day, or in moments when you feel disempowered. Repetition is where we change our mind's program.

Attraction

Our thoughts and words create our reality before our behaviors do. We must learn to harness our self-talk in a way where we speak only what we wish to manifest. We want to speak about the opportunities that are in front of us, how capable we are of achieving any goal that we wish; repeating affirmations that empower us to embody our future ideal self, and to allow our words to attract the magical synchronicities on behalf of the universe.

You must take these guiding steps that are necessary in creating the life you want. You may not feel you are worthy of success or love today. You may not at this moment believe yourself when you create an empowering dialogue in your head, and you may feel like this is stupid hippie bullshit. That's okay. Trust in the process. I promise you, this hippie bullshit works. There is science behind speaking the life you want with positive intent through repetition. There is power in trusting the process and doing the work. If the narrative that is running your mind disempowers you, then it's time to take control and choose different thoughts and approaches, in order to get to a place where you speak to yourself like your best friend, like a teammate, as if you loved yourself. This can change everything. Positive and empowering self-talk will change the quality of people, the quality of experiences, and the results that attract to you.

What are some negative self-talk phrases that often go through your mind? Reframe those phrases to be more empowering and positive. This helps you gain awareness of the different dialogues between the Inner Villain and the Inner Hero.

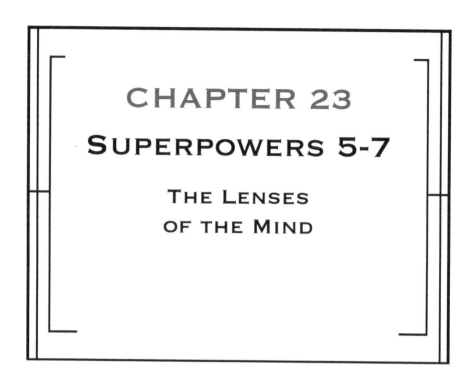

CHAPTER 23
SUPERPOWERS 5-7
THE LENSES
OF THE MIND

The lenses of the mind

In this section, we will talk about the lens through which you see the world. I tell myself every day, "It doesn't matter what you look at. It matters what you see." We get to CHOOSE what we see by deciding what lenses we want to wear. It's common to find people who believe that the type of lenses depend on the quality of the people we are around, or events that we experience. This way of thinking traps people into a conditional reaction pattern. In contrast, I believe the quality of lenses we put on determines the type of people or events that we experience. This is more of a responsive and intentional way of thinking; decided before coming into contact with anyone or anything. It takes practice to shift into this unconditional way of viewing the world, but it pays off when you embody this way of being.

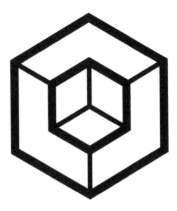

Superpower #5: Perception

This next superpower will enhance the lens through which you see the world. Remember, if you change the lens, then the world will change. It must, as each of our lenses is an illusion. Change the illusion, and everything else will change around you. It doesn't matter what you look at, it only matters what you choose to see.

Just because you are used to experiencing or seeing the world through your core lenses does not mean it is true, nor does it mean it has to stay that way forever. We interpret reality through practiced beliefs, ideologies, habits, likes, dislikes, influences, religion, parents, school, and more. You get to choose your lenses. The cool thing about perception is that everyone has perception, and no matter what that might be, it shapes who they are and how they show up. Your perception is your reality and no one else's. This is such a dominant trait as to who we are as human beings, and a collective that sometimes we are not aware of this solid foundation.

The external world may seem real since we use our senses to interpret it, but in actuality, it's an illusion. Our external world is a mirror of the truth from within. The quality of our inner world directly affects how we interpret the external world. We cannot control external stimuli, but we can ALWAYS control how we respond by being who we are and how we show up. This comes from the perception in which we see any situation, and this perception starts inside and through the lenses we choose. Keep in mind that most of the world does not consciously choose its lenses and is constantly reactive. People believe that the reason they feel a certain way is because of what's happening externally. Still, when you are conscious of this superpower, then you understand that you always have the power to perceive life in a way that reflects your values, uplifts you, and gives you meaning in a way where you find appreciation, and get to decide to respond consciously. This is the power of perception.

Perception is ultimately your mind's projector. A projector's job is to project a sequence of images on a screen. Depending on the reel inserted in that projector, the audience will see a specific movie. This is the same thing that happens to you when you put on a certain lens. You will experience a sequence of images on the forefront of your mind (movie screen) called reality, but it's only a perspective that is coming from the lens (movie reel). The lens represents the ideas and beliefs you have that interpret reality. When you implant the movie reel of ideas and beliefs in your mind (the projector), it seems like you are experiencing reality. Depending on what the director wants the audience to see will depend on the quality of the audience's experience. You are the director, the audience, and the projector in this example of perception. Most people are unaware of this truth. They become stuck in the prison of a movie directed by someone else. They live in an illusion because they don't realize they have the power to change the movie at any point they wish.

Let me break this down in another way by using a real-life example. I grew up in a religious and strict home. It gave me a perspective based on what I learned from my parents, church, and school. These were my directors, and they told me what to look for in life, which caused me to see certain experiences specifically. I would surround my lens with, "Am I good enough? If I fail, will I still be loved? Don't do that, because that's not what a good Christian would do."

I saw everything in my life with a certain frame of reference because my lens had ideas and beliefs attached to it, which projected certain images onto my life experience. When I changed the reel or lens through how I saw the world, how I saw God, how I saw myself; new images appeared. I became the director, and when I did, God became bigger, and so did my potential. No longer did I see right and wrong or failure as part of my experience, but I reframed them—how can I learn from this? I saw opportunities rather than fear. My life changed when I became the director and put in the appropriate reel to experience the life I wanted to see.

We decide to keep the perspective of our external world, or we can decide to be the hero of our life and be the director behind the lenses. What type of reality are you experiencing? How can you project a different reality and remove the illusion of your life?

Steve Jobs was the director of his life by changing his perspective. He wrote,

"When you grow up, you are told that the world is the way it is and your life is just to live your life inside the world. Try not to bash into the walls too much. Try to have a pleasant family life, have fun, save a little money. That's a limited life. Life can be much broader once you discover one simple fact that everyone around you are people who are no smarter than you. And you can change it. You can influence it. Once you learn that, you'll never be the same."

What does your lens look like? How do you interpret the world around you? What does that tell you about your beliefs? Create an ideal lens you wish to wear, and describe it with detail in your journal.

Superpower #6: Appreciation

Each superpower that you study in this book is transformational. Appreciation though, could be the one that changes your life the most. We have learned about the power of perception. While that superpower will change the way you see the world by putting on new lenses, appreciation is a power that amplifies perception and directs it to see more of the things that are going right in your life, rather than what are lacking.

Appreciation is the recognition and enjoyment of the wonderful qualities of someone or something. Appreciation is one of the highest forms of emotion that you can tap into. Everything that we think, feel, and do is energy with a specific vibrational resonance level. When you spend your time expressing appreciation, your energy or vibration will rise. Choose to see the bright side of all situations. When appreciation is a superpower, you can find something to be grateful for in the good and in the bad, win or lose, in our successes and failures, in love and in heartbreak, in life and in death. You can see opportunities to learn and grow when you're looking through the eyes of appreciation. Plant the seeds of appreciation in every area of your life. Water and care for these seeds by expressing genuine appreciation, heartfelt appreciation that shines through your actions. It won't take long until you see things shift in your life and reap the fruit of this superpower.

Our mind is an amazing mechanism. What we look for is what we see. There is a part of our brain called the Reticular Activating System (RAS). You trigger this part of the brain by telling it what to look for. This is for efficiency and focus, as there are so many objects in the world that can stimulate our senses. It's important to drown out the distractions. So what are you telling your brain to look at? The answer correlates to what you see throughout your day. Is it a reason to feel blessed and grateful, or a reason to be upset or feel defeated? We can practice and develop this.

Think back to a time when you were going to buy a new car? Let's say it's a Toyota Tacoma. When you make that choice, your brain sees every Toyota Tacoma on the road. Tacomas didn't show up out of nowhere. They were always there but you didn't notice them, because you were not looking for them when you drove. Your RAS was not told to pay attention. Your brain cannot focus on all the surrounding cars, or the names of all the businesses you pass by, the license plate numbers of each car or the people on the sidewalk—but your brain does. There is too much stimulation to internalize everything that the brain witnesses.

Your brain uses its mind power to focus on what you make as a priority in your experience. If you decide to use your mind power to set your RAS on a specific subject while you are driving to work today; let's say the people walking on the side of the road, then you will see the 100 people on the sidewalk and the details about them. They are always there, but you didn't see them.

We have the power to set our RAS to whatever we want in each subject. This brings me to the superpower at hand, appreciation. Imagine if appreciation is what you focus on when you interact with people, or the experiences you have throughout your day. How different would your life be? Appreciation is one of the highest vibrations you can embody. Rather than looking for all the things that go wrong in your life, or why this person pissed you off, or getting angry because you are stuck in traffic, try to see what you can appreciate in that moment. The more you focus on being grateful, the more the universe will show you what to be grateful for.

Remember, the people on the sidewalk were always there—you just didn't notice them. The Toyota Tacomas are out there, driving on the road every day, but you just weren't looking for them. There are infinite things to be grateful for in every moment. Adjust your perception and focus to look for them so you can see them. This alone can change your life. Make appreciation a priority above all else and you will see that you have more of an abundant life. It was abundant all along—you just didn't notice.

What things in your life have you been taking for granted? Make a list of 100 things you are grateful for?

Superpower #7: Visionary

This is my favorite superpower. To be a visionary is having the ability to dream up or create different future realities in your mind, then actualize them. We all have this magical gift to think into the future, dream beyond our current reality through our imagination, and then strategize how to take actionable steps to achieve this dream. When being a visionary is your superpower, you can take what is created in the mind's eye and mold it into physical reality.

Someone created everything that you see around you. Before that, it was a thought. Someone had to take that thought, and then make it real. This is the most magical aspect of the human mind. The key component to this superpower is imagination. Imagination is a boundless, limitless, and timeless experience of the creation of a reality conjured within the mind's eye.

The amazing thing about imagination is the fact that when you are using it, everything is imaginary. As in, you are putting images in your mind's eye that are in a non-physical world or dimension. It is a reality in your mind. People forget this when they are using their imagination. If you are thinking of a future experience, you are using your imagination, because the future does not exist yet. So why is it when we are using our imagination while looking into the future, do we put our limiting beliefs into that future reality? It doesn't exist, yet we inject our fears, worries, insecurities, limits onto why something won't happen. We project problems and so many other hurdles that hold us back inside of this imaginary future reality. You don't have to add any of those when using your imagination. If you can't even imagine a life without blocks and limiting beliefs in a fantasy world, how do you expect to live it in the physical world?

When we use our imagination, we need to treat it with the respect that it deserves. This is a magical power that the best visionaries in history, such as the Wright Brothers, used in inventing the plane, Henry Ford and the automobile, Thomas Edison and the light bulb, and Elon Musk and his desire to travel to Mars. They use their imagination to create a vision of limitless possibilities and then take steps to actualize their dreams. They didn't use their imagination to stop them from dreaming big, instead they used it to dream REALLY FUCKING BIG. This is the key to creating a better future for yourself and the world.

There is a 7-step process in becoming the ultimate visionary which you can learn more about through my online course. Until then, here are the 7 steps.

Step 1: Set a point of destination

Before traveling, you must know where you want to go. Create a sense of direction. Make sure to not be afraid to dream really fucking big. This destination can be an internal quest, a career, or a family. Whatever it is, know what you want. If you don't know what you want, then how can the universe know what to give you? Visionaries know what they want and understand where they are going.

Step 2: Define your why

Why do you want to travel to that destination? When you get there, how will you feel? What will life look like? The stronger the why, the better. The more clarity you have around the purpose of your destination while having a strong emotional charge, the more the destination will pull you in that direction. Having a powerful fire within your desires will keep you going when the journey gets tough.

Step 3: Create a theory

How do you think you will get there? Who will you have to become? What do you need to learn? In what areas do you need to ask for help? When creating a bigger dream than your current reality, you most likely don't know how to achieve it yet. So you must make up a theory of what it will take for you to get there. It's okay that you are not the version of yourself you need to be, nor do you have the know-how yet. That is why a theory is important in order to give yourself an idea of how to get there. The theory does not mean it is a plan set in stone, but something to practice, experiment with, and adjust as you move forward.

Step 4: How does the journey look and feel?

How would you like to handle challenges, people, and successes while on the way to this destination? I say this all the time. "The achievement of your goals is not as important as WHO you become in achieving your goals." So who are you becoming on the way to your destination? We are all travelers through space and time. When traveling, people have unique experiences. Some enjoy going to the airport, checking in their bags, and flying to their destination. Some people hate the process entirely and want to snap their fingers and appear at the destination. Anyone that has traveled to another country knows the challenges that go along with it. It's not a relaxing vacation it's an adventurous journey. How you perceive the journey is important. When being a visionary is your superpower, you see the journey or process as exciting, fun, playful, loving, empowering, and inspiring with gratitude. You look to learn from mistakes and see the bigger picture without getting caught up in the little hiccups along the way. You find peace from within and have faith that everything will work out how it's supposed to. These are empowering ways to look at the journey.

Step 5: Make a Move

"A Journey of a Thousand miles, begins with one step." - Lao Tzu.

After you have completed Steps 1-4, it's time to make a move. Don't wait. Take action now. It's not about taking leaps towards your goals, but consistent steps. Progress over perfection. Eventually, there will be a compound effect in which momentum will move you forward. Stagnation is the biggest dream killer. What is your first step forward?

Step 6: Adjust to the terrain and repeat the process

Creating a route from looking at a two-dimensional map is the theoretical aspect of the visionary's journey, but it will differ from traveling the three-dimensional life terrain. Adjust to roadblocks, mountains, other people, by developing skill sets, learning better routes, weather, endless fear and so on.

As a visionary, it's inevitable to run into challenges along your journey. Rather than getting caught up in the discouragement of the challenges, feel empowered to learn and adjust to anything that gets in your way. You are a badass, my friend. The external circumstances can't stop you because you are a hero, and you have your sights on a vision that inspires you with the more steps you take towards your destination. Your peace comes from within, so the terrain cannot stop you. Learn from what is in your way, face your fear, create space to develop a new theory or strategy, but don't give up. You are the only one on your journey that can stop you. So make sure you don't get in your way. Adjust to the terrain and then repeat the process. See if your vision still aligns with your why, and if you need to adjust your destination, this is the time. Continue to repeat this process, Steps 1-6, until you arrive at your destination and create a new vision for yourself.

Step 7: Inspire others along the way

"Vision without action is merely a dream. Action without vision just passes the time. Vision with action can change the world." - Joel A. Barker.

Many people have dreams but don't act on them. Sometimes all they need is a little inspiration and someone giving them permission to pursue their dreams. You can be that person for them. Inspire others to be a dreamer and encourage them to make a move. This is how visionaries change the world. You are already doing it by being here. If I can do it, then anyone can, I promise.

Return to your Transformational AHA! journal entry. Apply the 7-step process to be the ultimate visionary by rewriting what you plan to receive from implementing the superpowers.

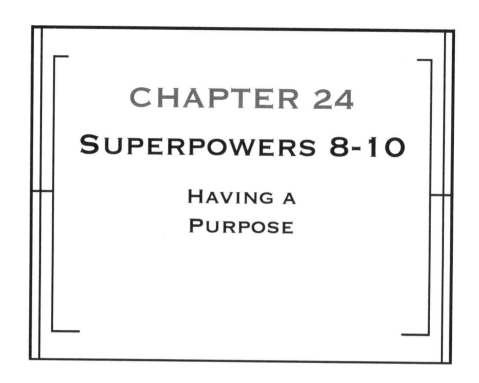

CHAPTER 24
SUPERPOWERS 8-10

HAVING A
PURPOSE

Having a purpose

What's the point of changing your life? Why would you even want to become the hero of your journey? There is a deep why behind these questions, and I'm asking you to explore this why? To change your life on a long enough timeline, you MUST have a burning passion inside your soul to keep you moving forward when life gets tough.

I'm encouraging you to discover your purpose. We all have a purpose inside of us. Not everyone on this earth is here to solve world hunger, promote peace, take us to the moon, or find the cure for cancer, but everyone is here for something, and it's our duty to uncover what that something is.

This next section is all about a purpose-driven life, and how to influence yourself and others to embody purpose in every aspect of day-to-day life. Don't be afraid to ask: What is my purpose? Why am I here? What drives me? How can I lead better within my purpose? The answers will come. Having an immense purpose, spirituality, drive, and leadership is how visionaries actualize their dreams.

Superpower #8: Spirituality

I have a definition of spirituality that may be contrary to its traditional definition. Spirituality is an intimate personal relationship within yourself that brings out purpose and passion for something bigger than yourself.

We are all non-physical spiritual beings living in a physical world having a human experience. How we decide to connect and express our spiritual selves will reflect the type of human experience we have in our lifetime, and the impact we have on the surrounding people. Most people interpret spirituality as being religious. This is not the case, though, as being religious does not always mean that you are spiritual, nor does being spiritual mean you are religious. You can be both, but because you are one doesn't mean you are the other. While spirituality is more about a personal relationship, a set of laws often guides religion in how to practice.

We can have spiritual experiences in many moments of life, such as the artist who spends 12 consecutive hours immersing herself in her painting. The janitor cleaning the elementary school halls feels a deep passion for serving the staff and students. To be in tune with a spiritual moment, you must recognize what lights you up inside. You only know this by spending intimate and quality time within yourself, and to know yourself on a deeper level. The more you explore your inner world, the more you will feel the infinite love within yourself. Your passions become amplified, and your desire to make an impact speeds up. When this happens, you take steps towards a purpose that you are passionate about that is bigger than yourself, because spirituality is not contained in your vessel. It's everywhere. When I say bigger than yourself that could mean a higher power, providing for your family, or it could serve children in an elementary school. It is bigger than just worrying about you. Service becomes a central part of your life, and sharing your passions with others is more important than surviving for yourself. The more spiritual you become, the more your life will radiate love. Spirituality comes from within, but it is around each of us. The deeper you go will guide you more toward being the hero of your life with a fiery passion unlike any other.

One more aspect of spirituality I would like to point out is the power of presence. When you immerse yourself in the present moment, everything around you disappears. You become entirely in flow with the present moment of the eternal now. The deeper you connect with your spirituality, the more you can embody these moments in your daily life. I live for these moments.

How have you viewed spirituality in your life? What does your spirituality look like? How can you enhance this superpower in your life?

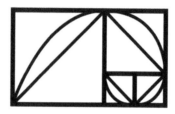

Superpower #9: Drive

Desire + Persistence + Resilience = Drive

Drive is an important aspect in accomplishing your dreams. The Inner Hero is more consistent than anything else in this universe. That part of yourself knows what you want and how to get there. Connecting to your personal Inner Hero will give you the guidance, and the steps to take in each chapter of your life.

The first part of the equation is the level of desire you have created around your purpose. This level of desire will determine the level of drive that you will possess. It's important to know that every elite athlete, actor, actress, writer, and leader had an unmovable drive for what they were looking to accomplish. To develop a strong drive, you must have a strong want. The quality of your "want" correlates to the quality of your purpose. You must uncover what lights your belly on fire when you think about it.

You can't expect a fiery drive if you have small goals. Your will to accomplish small goals will distinguish your flame, but when you create massive dreams, your drive will create a burning desire within your being. You will change everything in your life to align yourself with BECOMING the upgraded version you need to BE, and only then will you have a big enough drive to see your dream to fruition.

How is drive developed past having a massive dream? You understand obstacles will ALWAYS come into your experience. It's inevitable. You must never give up, though. The second part, persistence, is a key component to developing a passionate and fiery drive. You must adhere to daily practice in order to get better at your craft. When I say the word practice, I am not referring to doing something repeatedly while hoping you will get better. You will stay helplessly average if you practice bad habits, but you can become extraordinary if you have habits that have an intentional deep practice intertwined within them. Keep going. Don't give up. Repetition is important.

The third part of the equation to create an unshakable drive is to be resilient. This means that you will hit roadblocks, fall down, and fail repeatedly, yet you get yourself up by learning from the challenges you faced. Challenges are opportunities to learn and grow. If you can see challenges through this lens, you can get excited when they show up in your life, because you know you level up when you solve the problem at hand.

What is something in your life where you have an immense drive? How can you fan that flame?

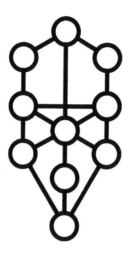

Superpower #10: Leadership

To live a purpose-filled life, it's necessary to develop your leadership skills into a superpower. The question is not whether you are a leader, but how well do you lead when you are in that role? Are you aware that you are a leader? The reality of leadership is that we are ALL leaders: mother, father, big brother, aunt, friend, co-worker, boss, mechanic, entrepreneur, cashier, dog groomer, athlete, or anything else. We are a leader of something, or someone, at different moments in our day. When we are aware of these moments and step into that role, we can lead more effectively and confidently.

Also, we are ALL followers. The greatest leaders of our time know when it's appropriate to lead, when it's time to follow, and by who. Great leaders follow others who are more capable in certain areas. They are coachable and always learn to improve so that their family, team, organization, or community improves. The most important part of being a leader is that they empower others to lead, as we are all leaders of leaders, even if some leaders are not yet aware of it.

The most loving and powerful leaders have a few common qualities.

Here are five.

Lead by example

Leaders lead by example. They don't have the mentality of "Do as I say, not as I do." They instead say, "Learn from what I do, as it follows what I say." I have always loved the quote from Gandhi, "Be the change you wish to see in the world." It's about BEING the change through your embodiment. Leaders take accountability for when things go wrong, and for that, their team is more willing to take accountability. Leaders are growth-oriented and are always looking for opportunities to learn from their failures, no matter how small or big. This teaches their team how to embrace failure rather than fear it. Leaders empower themselves first, and through that empowered state of being, they empower the people around them.

Sense of Direction

Leaders know where they are going. They have a powerful sense of direction because they know where the destination is. They are visionaries and have theories on how to execute their plan. People are more willing to follow someone with a clear picture of where they are going more than someone who lacks that clarity.

Clear communication

Leaders can articulate the direction they see to others. They have emotional intelligence and recognize how to speak with their team, family, or friends with direct honesty, compassion, and clarity. Great leaders move people into an empowered state of consciousness through their words and actions. They can create and communicate clear goals and action steps to accomplish those goals. Communication is a key to being a powerful leader and for building momentum toward the desired destination. The best leaders use their communication skills to challenge others and hold them accountable to their goals. Leaders can achieve this through inspiration and empowerment without being confrontational.

Disciplined in the process

Leaders are disciplined and focused. They stay on the path without being easily distracted or pressured. They know what they want and become what is necessary to accomplish what they want. They stay true to their values and hold themselves and their team to higher standards, understand that there is a process, so that no one gets negatively affected by the day-to-day challenges. Leaders create boundaries and structure to accomplish their goals, and help lead others in that same way, showing up day-after-day, disciplined to a high level of enthusiasm, and achieving unseen amounts of work effort towards the goals at hand. Leaders are always looking for new ideas to better the team, whether or not it's their idea. Their ego is not about being right, but about what is best.

Service to others

The best leaders are the ones who serve first. The more you give value and serve your family, team, employees, customers, neighbors, or friends, the more you get back. When you put service first, people trust you and want to mirror your efforts. Leaders who serve first are more fulfilled rather than leaders who are out for their own self-interest. This is an intelligent and loving way to lead, built around a purpose. Another aspect of service is bringing awareness to the surrounding people. As leaders, we want to empower our teams to lead, and bringing awareness to them in this area can be an extremely powerful service to whoever we are leading.

The more you develop your leadership into a superpower, the more confident you will become. We are here to be leaders of leaders. Empower each other to lead more lovingly and follow more intelligently. Leaders lead in their own life first, and through that example, others follow. Look for people in your life who are already doing this and emulate them. Leaders have mentors that inspire them to be better.

If we all embodied the understanding of leading ourselves first, as we are ALL leaders, then imagine the powerful transformation that would happen in our culture. Taking on that responsibility is life changing, not only for yourself but also for those around you. Lead in small ways and build to leading in big ways. They are both the same because, "How you do anything, is how you do everything."

Review the five qualities of a leader, then journal what it would look like to be the ideal leader of a specific area of importance in your life. Where do you believe you need improvement to bridge the gap from where you are now to where you become an ideal leader?

CHAPTER 25
SUPERPOWERS 11-12

UNCOVERING THE
INNER HERO:
YOUR TRUE NATURE

Uncovering the Inner Hero: Your true nature

Our Inner Hero is the Source of the true nature of our being. We were created, as everything in this universe was created. Something in the beginning of time eventually expanded to the creation of you and me through a long and slow process.

The Inner Hero is that source of All That Is. There are a few qualities that this Energy possesses, for example love and forgiveness. The Inner Hero does not stop here, as this part of ourselves and the universe are always expanding and evolving. The Inner Hero is completely unconditional, infinite, and omnipresent. When you discover the Inner Hero for yourself, you witness how extraordinary you can become. This process is more of an uncovering or a remembering rather than a discovery.

Your Inner Hero has been there since the beginning, and in most cases, we have covered that part of ourselves in layers of insecurities, traumas, anger, and resentment. The more layers you can peel off, the more you will uncover this beautiful part of yourself. When you uncover the inner truth, you will uncover the fact that the Inner Hero is everywhere, in everything around you, all at the same time. This connection will disintegrate the illusion you have been living in and allow yourself to wear upgraded lenses.

Superpower #11: Love

Love is the only work that we need to do along this journey. It's cliché, but it's true. To be more specific, we are all on a journey of self-love. This isn't an egoic type of love, or a materialist type of love, but I'm referring to the natural order of being whole. There are multiple components when talking about the subject of love: Self, relational, and universal.

1. Self-love

This refers to the vessel you live in. Your vessel is your home. It is the home where you have lived your entire life, and it is the home where you will live for the rest of your life. How are you taking care of your home? What type of guests do you allow in your home regarding the quality of thoughts, self-narrative, food, music, books, podcasts, and movies? If we loved ourselves, wouldn't we want to make sure we were filling up our vessel with things that uplift us and empower us, and accept nothing less?

Loving ourselves means we are consistently spring cleaning. We are cleaning out the dark corners of our house and attic that are holding trauma, outdated beliefs, and negative self-talk. This is part of the work for maintaining a loving home for ourselves.

We must also focus on filling up our cup first. If we have an empty cup, then how are we supposed to fill anyone else's cup with love? This type of love for ourselves and others cannot be sustained. You must focus on filling up your cup first by loving yourself and doing the things that give you energy, rather than doing things that take away from your energy. Things that add to your energy are exercising, reading, journaling, getting sunlight, getting time alone, sufficient nutrition, spending time in nature, having purpose, doing difficult things, and so much more. To fill our cup efficiently, we must set boundaries, even if those boundaries include how you deal with your spouse, kids, or friends. When our cup is full, we can love others with more capacity.

Self-love has nothing to do with what you do, but knowing who you are. You are connected with your Inner Hero, whether you are aware of it or not. Therefore, it is important to shed off all the layers and distractions that have been accumulating throughout your life, so that you may uncover this unconditional, loving part of yourself. It's been there from the beginning and it will be there till the end. You are already perfect and loved. It's your true nature. This is the ultimate truth! Are you able to accept it, or are you going to fight for all the reasons this isn't true? You get to decide. The more you accept this, and the less you judge yourself for all the reasons you think you fall short, the more joy you will experience in your life, and the more love you will shine on yourself and others.

2. Relational love

This type of love seems like it is about others, but this is a secondary manifestation of the quality of self-love you radiate. Relational love is how well you can connect and love others. Most people think we should love people based on how they treat us or others. This is not the case. You can love others unconditionally, despite their actions. This does not mean you need to engage with toxic people, nor condone their behaviors. I don't encourage tolerating abuse, and spending time in a space that projects negative energy of any kind. What I am encouraging is, how well can you love the unlovable? The more you can understand the fact that each of us connects to the same source, the same oneness, the same Inner Hero, then the more we can connect with the true wholeness of love. If we can understand that everyone functions on different levels of consciousness, one is not better than the other, they are different; then we can see that they are only functioning within the lenses in which they experience the world. The key to relational love is to accept each person for who they are without judgement. I couldn't agree more with Shakespeare who wrote, "Nothing is good or bad, but thinking makes it so."

Our lenses in which we see the world and the people are only reflections of ourselves. The more you can love yourself without judgment expands your ability to love others without judgement. If you are perfect as you are and you connect to this greater part of yourself known as the Inner Hero, then wouldn't it make sense that other people are perfect as they are, and also connected to the same Inner Hero? This can be hard for some people to accept when you look at all the horrific things that people can do to others, but it is only because they have a different program. It is because they don't have the level of consciousness to remember who they are. We can't allow other people's actions to be an excuse for us to not love them. It's easy to love loving people, but what about the unloving people? They are extensions of us, so to love ourselves, we must learn to see a way to love them as well. Any ill will or judgements we pass to others, no matter what behaviors they engage in, we pass on to ourselves. To love others unconditionally is to be whole in our self-love.

3. Universal love

You can probably imagine where this one is going. If we are truly one, then every person, every animal, every plant, every rock, every experience, and everything else is an extension of us. We are a single drop in the ocean, yet that means we are the ocean. Being a part of the whole still means that you are also the whole. This is consciousness. We are a piece of the whole, and there are many parts of the whole. We are making up the ocean of consciousness.

This is the Inner Hero, a part of consciousness that lives within us, and we get to connect with it in any moment or experience. When we can come into this awareness, we connect with the wholeness of the collective consciousness. This space is infinite and ever expanding. When we can love each of the universal parts of this consciousness, we become whole with our own consciousness. Every part of the whole is intrinsically experiencing the universal whole. Consciousness is experiencing different angles, perspectives, and parts of itself within each part. Each part plays a role, and we must learn to play our individual role to the best of our ability. Your role differs from my role, yet they are equally important. If there were no drops of water from the ocean, then there would not be an ocean. Consciousness works the same way. Loving each of the parts brings you a deeper love for the whole.

Think about how the love superpower plays a role in your life. What would it look like if you could improve in these three areas of Love?

Superpower #12: Forgiveness

Forgiveness is the power of releasing anger, resentment, shame, guilt, or blame toward an experience or a person. Forgiveness is a big part of our spiritual journey. We cannot be whole if we are holding onto experiences, traumas, or resentment. The Inner Hero can take our burdens and transform them into meaning and growth. If we could trade perspectives with our Inner Hero, we would learn that there is no need to forgive anyone or anything, because the Inner Hero never holds onto any negative feelings. The moment has passed and the Inner Hero always lives in the eternal present moment of the now. There is no judgement of good or bad from the Inner Hero's perspective—it just is. For us to connect completely with the Inner

Hero, we must learn to let go of or release any past or present negative feeling toward a person or experience. Forgiveness is not about the other person, but it is for you.

We hold others with a certain level of expectation of how we wish to be treated and loved based on our level of consciousness of what that means for us. People or experiences can never fulfill that expectation, as their level of consciousness and what that means to them is completely different. People may do horrendous things to us, and for that, we blame them for why we cannot feel fully loved. Feeling the way you do is completely valid, but just because it is valid does not mean that it serves you by continuing to hold on to it. It's harming you. That past moment is holding you in a place of suffering. You must learn to let it go. Forgive them as their level of consciousness holds them apart from being a loving being, and causes them to do unloving things to themselves and others.

Forgiveness does not mean you tolerate abuse and toxicity from others. It means releasing the anger, resentment, or blame you are holding onto about an experience or a person. You don't need to see or speak to that person again. They don't need to apologize. You need to give it up and move on for you to be whole. This person or experience stores a certain energy in your body, and is taking up space in your home. Your vessel does not want this visitor to live with you any longer, and it's time to take ownership of this energy. It's time to evict this energy and let it leave your body. Let's move on, so that you can breathe again. Let's let it go, so that you can connect deeper with your Inner Hero. You cannot fully love yourself if you allow these energies to live within your vessel. Clean house, and move on, or else you will continue to blame, be resentful, and suffer as an outcome.

There is one more aspect of forgiveness that I would like to touch on, which is the most important part. The hardest person to forgive is the person in the mirror. Forgiving yourself. It's easy to feel guilty, shame yourself, beat yourself up for situations, or allow yourself to be treated a certain way by others. You may think you deserve this punishment, but this is not true, nor does it serve your Inner Hero. You must love and forgive yourself. This is key if you want to forgive anyone else. Tolerate nothing but love from yourself. This will build internal trust when you treat yourself with love and respect.

No matter what you have done, no matter who you have hurt, you must release this energy or else you will spend your time in a deep and dark pit of guilt and shame your entire life. You cannot change what happened in the past, but you can learn from it and make sure you do better in the future. To fully love yourself, you must forgive yourself. God has. It's your turn.

What do you need to forgive yourself for?

Who else do you need to forgive?

CHAPTER 26

SUPERPOWERS 13-15

ALIGNING WITH THE

INNER HERO

Aligning with the Inner Hero

When you uncover your Inner Hero, it's time to align with that part of yourself throughout your day. The more we can be in alignment, the more we will be in a flow state of consciousness. We match up with all of our desires. Aligning with the Inner Hero is achieved by integrating all of these superpowers and developing them daily. This is when you see a genuine change in your life. You will witness and experience synchronicities, and manifestations show up consistently within your workplace, community, relationships, finances, spiritually, and everywhere else. This is where your outer world reflects your inner world.

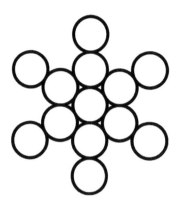

Superpower #13: Embodiment

The only way for you to align with your Inner Hero and possess each of the superpowers is through embodiment. They must live within your vessel. Each power must have a room in your home. Welcome each power into your home by integrating the skills you need to reinforce them to where they ARE part of you. Embodiment has to do with integration. It's not enough to know about the superpowers, but to integrate them into your day-to-day life with repetition and practice. You and the superpowers must become one-in-the same.

To embody the superpowers, I encourage you to experience each of them firsthand in as many areas of your life as you can. For example, if you were to embody the love superpower, you would experience love in every waking moment and in every situation and with every interaction. Only then will you align with love.

If you were to embody owning your reality, you would experience what that means in every waking moment and in every situation and with every interaction. To use embodiment, focus on one power at a time and reinforce that power through awareness and repetition. After a while, they will be ingrained in every cell of your body. This is the process of becoming. Going over each of these powers once will not allow you to embody them, but going over them ten times, or one hundred times, will certainly change the chemistry of your mind and state of being. Embodiment is your key to transforming into the hero of your own life.

What does it look like to embody each of these superpowers in your own life?

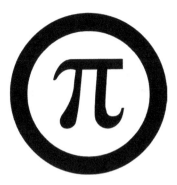

Superpower #14: Integrity

When you align with your Inner Hero, you will automatically start developing your integrity. This power is all about living in the truth of your alignment. Someone who has a high level of integrity engages in life with a high level of character. Who they are, is being reflected in all that they do. Someone with the superpower of integrity has clear values, a high sense of morals, and they are authentic. They follow through with what they say they are going to do, whether it is a minor task like taking out the trash, or a larger task like writing a book. When they say they are going to do something, they execute.

Authenticity is a big piece of integrity. They are the same person behind closed doors as who they are in front of people, honest with themselves and the people surrounding them, even if the truth hurts. They don't say something only to appease, but to stay in alignment with their level of integrity. This power is built upon a foundation of trust.

First build trust with yourself and then build that trust with others by following through. The best leaders in this world hold themselves to high standards of character and integrity. When you can embody integrity within each superpower, then you can be honest about where you are and what you need to work on within each space. Living in integrity within these powers will align you closer to your Inner Hero, which then brings you to the wholeness of your true essence.

Are you living within integrity? What do you need to address to live in an even higher state of character?

Superpower #15: Faith

Faith is the key to opening the door leading to our answered prayers, but faith can sometimes be misunderstood. If you grew up with a religious background, you were most likely taught to ask God for different things in your prayers. You were told to have faith that God will answer your prayers miraculously. Well, this is absolutely true in my experience, but there are more parts to the equation.

This is the equation for Answered Prayers.

A + B + CA = F (Asking + Belief + Courageous Action = Faith).

Here are a few verses around this subject from the Bible.

"You have not, because you ask not." - James 4:3

"Ask and it will be given to you; seek and you will find; knock and the door will be opened to you. For everyone who asks receives; the one who seeks find; and to the one who knocks; the door will be opened." Matthew 7:7-8

Let's break this equation down into bite-size pieces. "Ask and it will be given to you." To manifest the life that you desire, you must first have ASKED for what you want. Be clear in what you want, and be brave enough to ask for it, because I promise you, the universe wants to answer. How can your Inner Hero know what to give you if you never ask? This part of the equation can be scary. We don't give ourselves permission to ask for what we want, because if we ask and our prayer is unanswered, then we feel let down and discouraged. Sometimes we feel silly or undeserving to pray for big manifestations, so we only have little asks. God wants to give you your heart's desires. Don't be afraid to ask!

Next we must have BELIEF. Not any type of belief, but a belief of knowing. Know that the desire that you have asked for has already been answered. This is how it works. As soon as you ask a question in a non-physical realm, your manifestation is answered, but there is a buffering of time and space for it to show itself in our physical realm. It exists in a different vibrational reality. Know this, and seek for the feeling and uncovering of the dimension in which that manifestation lives. "Seek and you will find." You would only seek something if you knew you would, at some point, discover.

The last piece of the equation is, "Knock and the door will be answered." This is where COURAGEOUS ACTION takes place. I don't mean timid action, wetting your toes before jumping into the ocean. No, I'm speaking of courageous actions. This is where you have a running start and jump headfirst into the deep end. Keep in mind I'm also not referring to reckless action, doing for the sake of doing. You have your desire in your mind, you have asked for it, you know you are going to receive it, and you are knocking on the doors of opportunity day after day with courageous action. If you do this repeatedly, learning from every action you take, readjusting, recalculating, smiling at every no that comes your way, then you are embodying what it means to have faith as a superpower.

It's only a matter of time until you are living within the vibrational reality of receiving your answered prayers. God matches the quality of faith that you emulate, so the more faith you have the more the universe will conspire to manifest your desires.

Take the formula $(A + B + CA = F)$, and apply it to your life.

A represents something you have asked for.

B represents the belief you have for what you asked for.

CA represents what courageous actions you need to take.

Add these together and describe the quality of faith you have for what you have been asking for.

Do you believe your equation will eventually lead to an answered prayer?

CHAPTER 27
SUPERPOWERS 16-18

BEING THE
INNER HERO

Being the Inner Hero

What happens when you awaken to your inner world, aware of the foundations of change, upgrading the lenses of your mind, discovering the fullness of your life's purpose, uncovering and aligning with the Inner Hero and the true nature of the universe? Everything in your life transforms and you and your Inner Hero become one. This last section is about being the Inner Hero.

Life is all about WHO you are, and by HOW you show up. When the superpowers become a part of your everyday life, you see changes all around you by the way you engage with life and everything within it. Here are some superpowers that will be enhanced when being the hero of your life is a part of how you show up daily.

Superpower #16: Attitude

Attitude is how a person carries oneself in any situation or experience through the alignment of their thoughts, feelings, and behavior. I have explained this process before, but I believe it's worth going over it again from a new angle; since your attitude directly correlates with how aligned you are with your Inner Hero, which is correlated with the results you see manifesting in your life. So let's break this down into bite-size pieces.

What does it mean to be aligned?

Alignment directly correlates to the results you are receiving in your life. Here is what alignment looks like when we break it apart.

Thoughts = What you think

Feelings = Emotions

Behavior = What you do

Attitude = How you show up

Results = Alignment

Thoughts are what you think.

"A man is literally what he thinks, his character being the complete sum of all his thoughts." - James Allen.

It all begins with your thoughts. Thoughts include, but are not limited to, self-talk, perception, identity, interpretation, beliefs, self-worth, control, ideas, and values. Depending on the quality of your thoughts will determine the quality of your emotions.

Feelings are the body's physical reaction to emotions. A thought-form literally releases chemicals in your body that create emotion. The emotion that you are experiencing then creates how you feel. Dr. Joe Dispenza says that we consider it a mood if you are feeling a certain way for a few hours or days. If you experience it for a week or two, then it's a temperament, but if you experience it for months at a time or years, it is now your personality. The way you feel day after day will determine the inspired actions you consistently take.

Behavior is your consistent action. When you take action, it directly reflects how you are engaging in life. These actions that are being performed by you are your functioning behaviors. The quality of your behavior determines the quality of how you show up in any situation or experience. We call this attitude.

Great leaders and influencers show up every day with positive attitudes, uplifting others, looking for solutions, and empowering themselves and everyone else around them. They are in alignment. Attitude is key to being fully alive. Your attitude amplifies the more you work on each superpower, building confidence and faith.

How do you carry yourself in situations and in experiences? What does that tell you about your attitude? What does that tell you about the alignment of your thoughts, feelings, and behaviors?

Superpower #17: Connection

Connection is the ability to synergize with others. Others may include intimate relationships, family, friends, strangers, community, company, coworkers, and yourself. The more you are being the hero of your life, projecting love and a positive attitude, then the more people will be drawn to you like a magnet. They may not understand why they feel exhilarated to be in your presence, but I will help you understand the reason. Positive energy is contagious. It is healing and empowering. When you are being the hero of your life, people will feel good around you because you amplify a vibrational frequency that feels good.

Let me say it in another way. You have heard of auras; an energy field that surrounds each of us? You can look at it as if you live in a big invisible bubble. The stronger your bubble, the more influence you have on the surrounding people. Let's say you are near a friend, so now, your invisible bubbles are entangled. The way energy works is that the vibrational frequency of the two bubbles merge. If you are the hero of your life, and you embody each of these superpowers with your attitude, then your bubble will feel superb and shift the other person's bubble.

The other person may not be aware of what's happening, but it's important for you to be consciously aware of how this works. The reason it's important is that you have been around people in the past with strong bubbles and they have unintentionally affected your bubble, negatively or positively. We all know the person at work who always has a rain cloud above them, and complains about how miserable life is. You feel a little less like the hero of your own life when in their vibrational field, but if you are aware of this bubble next time you are around them, you can amplify your own field so that they don't have a negative effect on you.

You have also been around the person at work who is always smiling and laughing. Their bubble feels fantastic to be around, which results in you feeling a heightened sense of state of being after you leave their presence. This is the power of connection.

How does your bubble affect those around you? Do people leave more empowered, loved, and whole? When you are the hero of your life, you will see how relationships shift into a positive state. You and the other person heal, forgive, connect, uplift, love, be vulnerable, and not judge each other. Your bubble is a safe space, and it draws people toward you, rather than feeling repelled. Connection is a natural result when you are the Inner Hero.

Do people enjoy being around you? How can you enhance this superpower in your life?

Superpower #18: Opportunist

When you stop looking for the outside world to save you and you readjust to the way you see the world, you notice things that you might have missed out on before. When you reset your reticular activation system to see opportunities, you see them everywhere. Being an opportunist is an absolute superpower. You see that every moment of life gives you an opportunity for something. You get to decide what that something is. When a challenge pops up, as they always do, you will see opportunities to grow, learn, release, forgive, love deeper, and develop one of your other superpowers.

When you are playing an extra or a supporting role in the movie of your life, you are waiting for someone or something to save you. When you become the hero of the movie of your life, you suddenly see that you have much more control than you could ever imagine. This is what it is like to see your life through the lenses of the opportunist. Think back and reflect on your life for a moment. Think about each of the opportunities that you have had to seize life's moments to their fullest. You cannot live a full life if you cannot see opportunities as they come and take action on them.

So many of us hide in our boxes of comfort. We don't like to move out of that space even if we see opportunities because it can be scary. To live life to its fullest, you must seize these gifts of growth and expansion that the universe puts in your path. It may be as simple as striking up a conversation with a stranger in the elevator by asking about their day, or finding the courage to ask your work crush out on a date. Maybe you have wanted to start a business, or learn about trading crypto, but it intimidates you. An opportunist takes risks, leans into being courageous, and learns how to make things work for them. We can each be an opportunist by adjusting our eyes when opportunity shows up.

A key component to being an opportunist is curiosity. Curious about people, curious about learning, about understanding, knowing more about your own self, about the world around you, about what possibilities or opportunities will show up for you today. Curiosity leads to opportunity. "What if? Why? What about? I wonder? What's your name? What do you do? What's next? Maybe there's another way?"

We don't know what we don't know, so if we walk around thinking that we know, rather than being curious about the people and world around us, then we will certainly miss out on the moments of opportunity.

Opportunities are everywhere in every moment. I promise. You can embody each of these superpowers, maybe not today, but you can decide that you WILL start today. You got this, and I believe in you.

How do you plan to be more aware of and take action on the opportunities that show themselves to you? What opportunities do you think will show up, when you implement these superpowers into your daily routine?

CONCLUSION
This is Just
the Beginning

Now that you have heard my story and learned how to develop your internal powers to uncover the Inner Hero, where do you go from here? I encourage you to go deeper. Your journey never ends. You can read this book 100 or 1000 times and you will discover something new each time.

I have repeated concepts in this book intentionally to reinforce the information into your subconscious. Through repetition, we change the program into one that we create for ourselves. We can change our lives if we see the opportunity, take courageous action towards our desired destination, trust the process, and do the work, because the work, works.

Daily, go deeper by practicing, developing, and being aware of each of the superpowers. Jump into my online courses and learn more wisdom on how to deepen your knowledge and connection to your Inner Hero. Join the community so you have a tribe on your same wavelength. Remember, you are the five people that you spend your time with. You can't imagine how much farther you can go by joining a conscious community. Take part in the online and live workshops and retreats to receive emotional impacts that produce life transformational results. Subscribe to *A Hero's Academy - AHA!* YouTube channel to receive weekly AHAs where I offer tips to enhance your life. Hear from other everyday heroes and how they took control of their lives.

For the goal you hope to accomplish, remember this truth: "Achieving your goal is not as important as WHO you become in achieving your goal." There are plenty of resources at your fingertips, but only you can decide whether you will capitalize on the opportunity to be the hero of your life. You get to decide.

You are not on this journey alone. There are endless people here with you. I am always on this journey with you. There are moments in my story in which everything clicks, and I am in complete alignment, but then, as life evolves, I must evolve. In those chapters of life, I said goodbye to the outdated version of myself, and said hello to who I was called to be.

Every chapter allows you the opportunity to see that this is the beginning of your life and from a new vantage point. Repeat the process by continuing to do the work, because the work, works. You can create the life of your dreams. I believe this to my core and have seen firsthand how the work has changed my life and countless others. If I can do it, anyone can, especially YOU. Continue to uncover the Inner Hero, and you too will know that this is the leading edge of your life. You are here for an extraordinary life. You only get the ONE, so what are you going to do with it now that you have the tools to make it great?

I can't thank you enough for taking the time to read this book, for investing in yourself, and for expanding the consciousness of our world. You are the ripple that changes the program for our future generations. It starts today. It starts now. It starts with you, by Uncovering the Inner Hero.

With all the love in my soul,

Jonathon Calhoun Dugan

ABOUT THE AUTHOR

Jonathon Calhoun Dugan was born and raised in Las Vegas, Nevada. Founder of A Hero's Academy LLC, he is an Inner Hero life coach, certified through iPEC (Institute for Professional Excellence in Coaching), a meditation instructor, and NFT (non-fungible token) enthusiast.

His mission in life is to help others connect deeper with themselves and actualize their inner potential. He loves traveling the world, creating meaningful moments with his partner Mackenna, and being a father of two little boys. If you would like to learn more about his NFT community, online workshops, coaching, and the meaning behind the symbols visit his website: https://aherosacademy.com.

To help bring awareness to Jonathon's mission follow Jonathon on Instagram @jonathon.dugan, tag him with a picture of you with this book, tag a friend who you believe will benefit by being the hero of their own life, and use the hashtag #TheInnerHero.

ACKNOWLEDGEMENTS

"If I have seen further, it is by standing on the shoulders of giants."
- Isaac Newton.

Thank you to the ones who have come before me, who are with me now, and who are on their way into my life to help guide me along my journey. I love you all.

Michael, thank you. You have been my greatest teacher. Through you, I live a deeper life.

My Coaches, thank you. You know who you are. Each of you have guided me in major breakthroughs during my lows.

Surrender Crew, thank you. Since our first meeting in Phoenix, I was hooked. You are the real ones. You have challenged me, and pushed me to greater heights.

You², thank you. Cheers to continued growth and learning every week. Each of you have held me accountable to completing this book.

Impact Theory University - Tom Bilyeu, thank you. You have inspired me to learn and be more than I am today. You have taught me to hold high standards for myself, and the people around me. You were my big brother during my darkest hour. Thank you. ITU Team, thank you. You make the community thrive. Your passion, dedication, and love is felt. ITU Community, thank you. People like you will change the world. Stay hungry, and keep serving.

Humans I Trust - Virginia, thank you. Creating this amazing movement has led many spiritual leaders to step into their ultimate power. Brad, thank you. Hosting the first HIT workshop in America took courage. Stepping out in leadership allowed me and others to receive an abundance of magic on that day. Destiny, thank you. Your intuition told me it was time to write this book. The next day I took action, and now it has manifested.

Pavel Stuchlik - NOAIAON, thank you. You are a modern day shaman. Your guidance has led me to some of my deepest healing.

Joey, thank you. Hours upon hours together reconfirms the old saying, Iron sharpens iron. I'm grateful for you introducing me to Carolyn.

Oxygen Publishing House - Carolyn, thank you. I started this publishing journey with zero knowledge and you have held my hand every step of the way. You are a true professional. Richard, my patient editor, thank you. Not only did you do an amazing job editing my book, you took your time to educate me so I can become a better writer.

My friends, thank you. You have helped me up every time I fell down. You have helped me laugh when I felt like crying. You held me when I was alone. You have unconditionally been my friends. Thank you.

Mom and Dad, thank you. You have taught me what it takes to be the leader of my home. I am grounded in spirituality, and seek endless wisdom from our Creator. There is value in having values. I live with integrity and character for I can gift these virtues to my family even when I am gone — I inherited these truths from you.

Kristine and Danielle, thank you. You have morphed from being my big sisters to my best friends. I love you and all that you are. You are gifts to this world and it's a pleasure watching you shine your light.

Brody, thank you. You know why they call you the man? Because you are the man! Keep being you, nephew. The world needs more Brody in it.

Mackenna, thank you. You came into my life exactly when I needed you. You have helped me love myself more through your example. You flow through life with deep ease and wisdom. Cheers to a long joyful life together. Thank you.

Greyson and Emerson, thank you. My sons, you have woken me up more than anyone else. You have empowered me to step up as a man. You have inspired me to live my dreams. You have healed me from my insecurities. I bask in our yesterdays, I soak up our todays, and I am giddy for your tomorrows.

Past Self, thank you. You could have given up at any point but instead you dug deeper. I'm proud of you.

Future Self, thank you. You are the footprints in the sand who have led the way.

Inner Hero, thank you. You have never left or forsaken me. You are my guiding light. You are love. You are healing. You Are—I Am.

Everyone else that wasn't mentioned, know that you are loved and appreciated. Thank you!